CRYSTALS

An Hachette UK Company
www.hachette.co.uk

First published in Great Britain in 2021 by
Godsfield, an imprint of
Octopus Publishing Group Ltd
Carmelite House
50 Victoria Embankment
London EC4Y 0DZ
www.octopusbooks.co.uk
www.octopusbooksusa.com

Distributed in the US by
Hachette Book Group
1290 Avenue of the Americas
4th and 5th Floors
New York, NY 10104

Distributed in Canada by
Canadian Manda Group
664 Annette St.
Toronto, Ontario, Canada M6S 2C8

ISBN 978-1-84181-499-5

A CIP catalogue record for this book is available
from the British Library.

Printed and bound in China

10 9 8 7 6 5 4 3 2 1

All reasonable care has been taken in the
preparation of this book but the information it
contains is not intended to take the place of
treatment by a qualified medical practitioner.
Before making any changes in your health
regime, always consult a doctor. While all the
therapies detailed in this book are completely
safe if done correctly, you must seek
professional advice if you are in any doubt
about any medical condition. Any application of
the ideas and information contained in this
book is at the reader's sole discretion and risk.

Publishing Director: Stephanie Jackson
Commissioning Editor: Natalie Bradley
Art Director: Yasia Williams-Leedham
Production Controller: Emily Noto

Project Editor: Clare Churly
Copy-editor: Mandy Greenfield
Designer: Leonardo Collina
Illustrator: Emilia Franchini

CRYSTALS

THE GUIDE TO PRINCIPLES, PRACTICES AND MORE

Lauren D'Silva

Contents

8 CRYSTAL DIRECTORY

1

ABOUT CRYSTALS

What Are Crystals?

A definition of a crystal is matter that is formed of a regular and orderly arrangement of atoms and molecules in a three-dimensional shape. This arrangement forms a box-like structure, which repeats to create a lattice. Matter that lacks a regular internal structure is termed "amorphous". Some of the stones we commonly refer to as crystals, such as obsidian, are technically not eligible for the term as they don't have the inner structure of a crystal.

The internal geometric structure of a crystal was proposed by a French schoolteacher, René Just Haüy, in 1784. He accidentally dropped a calcite crystal and noticed that the broken pieces all displayed a similar appearance. He concluded that the "elementary cells" making up the crystal must be geometric to produce this effect. He was close to the truth. Although atoms and molecules are not geometric shapes in themselves, they are arranged geometrically within a crystal.

There are only seven crystal systems, each classified by their angles of symmetry: cubic, hexagonal, tetragonal, trigonal, orthorhombic, monoclinic and triclinic. Some of these geometric shapes are apparent from the outer shape of the crystal – for example, pyrite is cubic, and cube-shaped pyrite crystals can be found; and beryl crystals, such as aquamarine, form hexagonal crystals and grow as six-sided pillars. Other crystals do not demonstrate their internal structure so obviously, although their interior geometry is always present. This remains the case where a crystal has been polished and tumbled (see page 167) or carved. When you hold a crystal, you are holding a piece of natural geometry.

Crystalline lattices can be extremely stable and long-lasting. The oldest crystal discovered so far is zircon, found in the Jack Hills of Western Australia, which has been dated as being 4.4 billion years old. To put its age in context, the Earth is only thought to have cooled enough to form a crust 4.6 billion years ago. Zircon is a hard crystal that resists weathering extremely well, which is why these crystals have been so enduring. A typical collection may contain some crystals that are 1 billion years old.

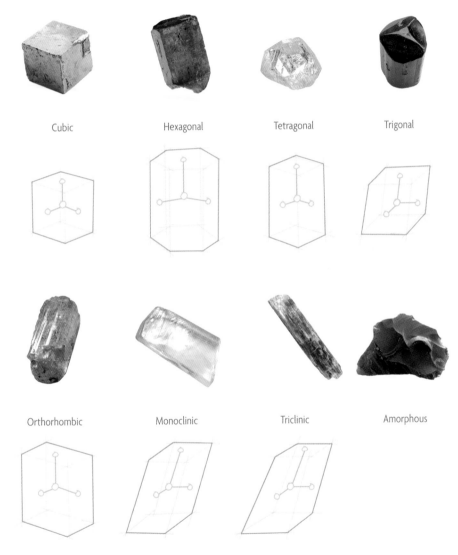

Cubic

Hexagonal

Tetragonal

Trigonal

Orthorhombic

Monoclinic

Triclinic

Amorphous

Our planet is slowly cooling, but it is still incredibly hot beneath the surface. It is believed that Earth's inner core is hotter than the surface of the Sun. All life exists on the cooled crust, which has a thickness of 8–40km (5–25 miles), with the thinnest parts beneath the oceans. The crust is very thin compared to the other layers of the Earth and comprises only about 1 per cent of the Earth's weight. An analogy often used is that the thickness of the crust can be compared to the skin of an apple. The Earth's diameter is almost 12,900km (8,000 miles) across. The mantle beneath the crust is estimated to be at least 2,100km (1,800 miles) thick. Erupting volcanoes give us a glimpse into the heat of the mantle and of the pressures within the planet. The outer core is believed to be completely liquid and molten, and made of iron and nickel; the Earth's inner core is solid and made of iron.

The Earth's crust is not stationary and inert, although it feels like it is most of the time. The crust is floating on the mantle, and the continents are slowly moving. The movements of the crust generate a dynamic and ongoing process in which rocks are drawn into the mantle to be melted and are then thrust up to cool and re-form. Rocks become molten magma at between 600°C and 1300°C (1100°F and 24000°F). Crystallization can occur when the temperature of a liquid falls beneath its melting point. In the case of water, this is 0°C, at which point ice crystals begin to form. If you have seen a snowflake with its six-sided shape, the crystalline nature of ice becomes obvious. Fortunately for us, rocks have a much higher melting point, otherwise life on Earth wouldn't exist.

Rocks that form from magma are igneous, getting their name from the Latin *ignis*, which means "fire". Igneous rock may cool very quickly – for example, when lava erupts from a volcano. These rocks will be fine-grained due to the limited time for crystallization to occur, or obsidian, a natural volcanic glass with no internal structure, may form. Other igneous rocks have a less violent birth and make slow progression toward the surface, taking thousands – perhaps millions – of years to cool. When the growing conditions are right, large and beautiful specimens can form. Examples of crystals that form in this way include emerald and aquamarine, peridot, topaz, tourmaline and most members of the quartz family.

When exposed to the surface of the Earth, rocks are subjected to weathering and erosion from the action of the Sun, water and wind. Over long periods of time they can be broken into tiny fragments, called sediment. These particles gradually accumulate and form layers, which are compacted by more layers forming above them. The growing weight of layers cements the particles together to form sedimentary rocks like sandstone, chalk and shale. Larger crystals can form within sedimentary rock – for instance, pyrite grows where the mud is rich in iron and sulphur. Malachite, chrysocolla and turquoise may form where there is copper present. Selenite crystallizes out of mineral-rich water underground, which is also classed as a sedimentary process.

A third type, metamorphic rock, is formed when igneous or sedimentary rocks become buried deep within the Earth's crust and are subjected to heat and great pressure, which transforms them. Examples of crystals found in metamorphic rock include lapis lazuli, garnet, kyanite and jade.

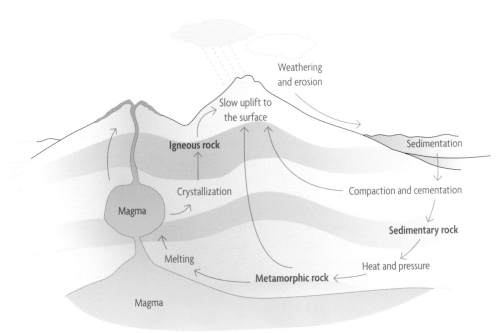

A Brief History of Crystals

Early humans started to use stones as primitive tools around 2.6 million years ago. The earliest "toolkit" was found in Africa and included rudimentary "hammers" and sharp flakes of stone for cutting. By 1.76 million years ago, humans were chipping at flints to shape axes, cutting tools and scrapers. Imagine for a moment what a difference these tools must have made to Stone Age life.

The Altamira cave paintings in Spain date back more than 35,000 years, but it is thought that grinding iron-rich rocks to create ochre pigment might be a much older practice. Ochre was sometimes used when preparing the body for burial. It is believed the pigment was not simply for decoration, but had magical and shamanic meaning for early humans.

In Ancient Times

We know that crystals were used ceremonially and for adornment in many ancient civilizations across the planet, including Sumerian, Egyptian, Grecian, Roman, Mayan, Incan and Chinese. Crystal jewellery is often depicted in the art of Ancient Egypt. Both sexes are shown wearing beaded collars, headdresses, belts and bracelets. Sometimes the figures are naked apart from their beads. Beaded and carved jewellery has been found in ancient tombs. These items were not simply decorative; they were believed to have the power to ward off evil and enhance the fortune of the wearer in the afterlife. The dead were often buried with a carved scarab beetle placed over their heart as a protective amulet to ensure their rebirth. Exquisite pectoral designs have been discovered crafted from gold and inlaid with stones, including lapis lazuli, carnelian and turquoise. The appearance of crystals was linked to the heavenly bodies: lapis lazuli represented the night sky full of stars, and the metal gold was symbolic of the Sun.

Cylinder seals from Mesopotamia made of precious gemstones, including lapis lazuli, serpentine and haematite, have been found dating back as far as 3,300 BCE. These were used to roll across the clay that sealed temple chambers, and were often carved with images of the gods.

The Epic of Gilgamesh is regarded as the world's oldest-surviving work of literature, containing Sumerian poetry from around 2,000 BCE. Within this epic poem the eponymous hero goes on a quest to find otherworldly jewel trees in the garden of the gods, which are described as being made of carnelian and lapis lazuli. Jewelled trees are a popular motif and make an appearance in several myths and legends. Within the ancient Jewish tradition of Kabbalah, the Tree of Life symbolizes the energy of all creation. The spheres of energy on the Tree are called *sephiroth*, translating literally as "sapphires".

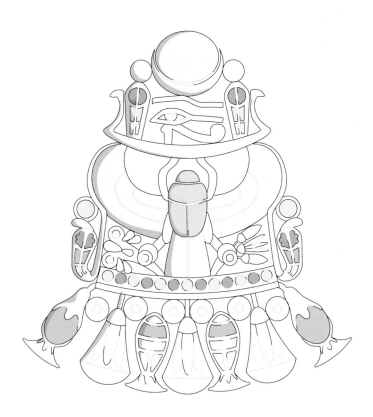

A Symbol of Spirituality

Crystals were widely believed to be sacred. Their beauty and the perfect geometric shapes of many crystals proved that they were gifts of the gods. The rulers of ancient lands would own the finest gems to mark their god-given power. The age-old practice of rulers wearing the most magnificent gemstones as a sign of their high status and authority to rule continues right through to the present day. The British Crown Jewels contain many outstanding and historically important gemstones.

Gemstones feature within the Bible in both the Old and New Testaments. In Exodus the jewelled breastplate of the high priest Aaron is described in some detail. The instructions for its creation were believed to have been given directly by God to Moses. The 12 gemstones of the breastplate represented the 12 tribes of Israel and were said to shine with light whenever God was present. The exact stones used are now a matter for debate, as some names have changed over time. For example, most modern interpretations list topaz as one of the gems, but it is thought this may in fact have been peridot. The high priest also wore two magical stones, called Urim and Thummim, over his heart. These are usually depicted as a white and a black stone. No one is certain how these stones were used, or what they were made of, but it is believed they were used by the high priest in judgement.

A vision of the New Jerusalem built upon the foundations of 12 gemstones is described in the New Testament Book of Revelations. The wealthiest medieval churches emulated this heavenly city by richly embellishing their interiors and decorating the vestments of their priests, chalices, crosses and other sacred artefacts with gemstones. Remains of saints were often housed in exquisite jewelled reliquaries, which reflected the heavenly blessings they were sure to be enjoying.

Magical Properties

Medieval alchemists were famed for their quest to turn base metal into gold. For this they needed the legendary Philosopher's Stone, which also had the power to rejuvenate the holder and bestow long life. The search for the Philosopher's Stone was called the *Magnum Opus* or "great work", through which the alchemists believed they would attain enlightenment.

It is believed that scrying in polished crystals (gazing into a reflective surface to gain psychic impressions) is a practice dating back thousands of years. John Dee was an occultist, seer and adviser to Queen Elizabeth I. The British Museum has his polished black mirror of obsidian in its collection, along with his smoky quartz sphere, called a "shew stone". His obsidian mirror was a sacred artefact that originated in Mexico. The Aztecs had a god of sorcery called Tezcatlipoca whose name translates as "smoking mirror". Aztec priests would have used the mirror for prophecy. John Dee was said to have used it to conjure up visions of angels.

Much folklore regarding crystals must have been lost, as it would have been passed on by word of mouth. Most healers would have been illiterate. During the era of the witch trials even those who could read and write would have been sensible to avoid making written records. There was a suspicion of anything "magical", and to be accused of witchcraft really was a mortal danger.

Crystal Healing

As well as sacred and magical uses, crystals have long been prized for their healing properties. The Indian system of Ayurveda is probably the world's oldest-surviving healing tradition. It is hard to say how far back it goes – some sources claim 5,000 years, others a more conservative 3,000 years. Ayurveda makes use of gemstones in healing and assigns astrological associations to the crystals.

Early medicinal uses of precious and semi-precious stones were often based around the appearance of the crystal and the principle of "like curing like", in a similar way to homeopathy today. Stones with red markings such as bloodstone would be used to stop bleeding, yellow stones might be used to treat jaundice, and so on. There is evidence that gemstones were being used medicinally in medieval times and were regarded as objects of power. The 12th-century abbess Hildegard of Bingen wrote a chapter about the therapeutic uses of gemstones in *Physica*, her book about healing.

Some scepticism regarding the healing power of crystals has probably always existed. In the 1500s the court jester of Emperor Charles V is reputed to have been asked what the properties of turquoise were. He quipped that if you were to fall from a high tower while wearing a turquoise ring, then the ring would remain unbroken! His wit, though scathing, serves to remind even firm believers in the properties of crystals that they shouldn't be seen as cure-alls.

A Status Symbol

Gemstones never went out of demand for adornment. Jean-Baptiste Mellerio was the jewellery designer for the 18th-century French court at the time of Marie-Antoinette. He is credited with the creation of acrostic jewellery, where the first letter of each gem spelled out a word. These jewels were sometimes used as gifts to declare secret love. Acrostic jewellery was fashionable in Georgian and Victorian England, where it was referred to as the "language of gemstones". Jewellery spelling DEAREST and REGARDS were popular as love tokens, at least among those who could afford them. REGARDS might be spelled out with Ruby, Emerald, Garnet, Amethyst, Ruby, Diamond, Sapphire.

Modern Uses

Modern technology has made great use of the properties of crystals. The first laser was developed by Theodore Maiman in 1960 using a ruby, creating a pure, intense laser beam of red light. Modern lasers now incorporate synthetic lab-grown gemstones, including diamonds, as these are "perfect", containing no impurities, and produce the accurate and precise rays of light needed for laser surgery.

The accuracy of quartz clocks and watches is due to the precise and predictable vibration of the quartz crystal, and modern computers have been built around the silicon chip. The basic material for the silicon chip is sand, which is silicon dioxide, also known as quartz.

Marcel Vogel was an IBM research scientist and the creator of the first liquid-crystal displays (LCDs). He was interested in subtle energies. Following a spiritual awakening in India, he started to experiment with quartz crystals. He found that he could amplify how a person was feeling by pointing a quartz crystal toward them, and the person would sometimes go into an altered state of consciousness. He began to use quartz crystals for healing and developed a specially faceted crystal, called a Vogel crystal, which produces a particularly coherent and precise beam of healing energy.

There has been a resurgence in the use of crystals for healing since the 1980s and interest in crystals has continued to grow. From being regarded as a "far-out" therapy, crystal healing has gradually become more mainstream and has many converts. Now those who enjoy crystals can be found in all walks of life, and for every person who speaks openly about crystals there are many more who quietly carry or wear crystals and believe in their power.

A Source of Spiritual Awakening

Some of those drawn to work with crystals have past-life memories of using them for healing in ancient times. The mythical civilizations of Lemuria and Atlantis are of interest to many crystal enthusiasts. Legend tells of huge crystals that were used in Atlantis as power stones and formed the foundation of sophisticated technology. It is believed that the misuse of their power led to the destruction of the land in an enormous cataclysm.

We cannot prove the existence of Atlantis or Lemuria, but we do know that the land masses of the Earth have changed over time. For example, only 8,000 years ago it was possible to walk from mainland Europe to the British Isles. The lost terrain has been called Doggerland. We know that some previously inhabited lands are now lost beneath the oceans. There are several candidates for the lost civilization of Atlantis. One is around the Greek island of Santorini, which is all that remains of a much bigger volcanic land mass. Others think it was located in the Caribbean.

It is thought that we are currently in transition from the astrological Age of Pisces into the Age of Aquarius. Each astrological Age is believed to last 2,160 years. It is predicted that the Age of Aquarius heralds immense change and contains the potential for humanity's spiritual evolution. This is what people are referring to when they speak of the New Age. Most people can see that this is indeed a time of great upheaval on the planet. Looking at the state of the environment, we see clear warning signs that humanity needs to change course as a matter of urgency. The warning contained in the legend of Atlantis becomes all too pertinent. We must take responsibility for our creations, as they have the potential to destroy us.

More people than ever are experiencing spiritual awakening and discovering the subtle realms that exist beyond the physical senses. Crystals are a part of this mass awakening. At this pivotal time, crystals can support us in recognizing and developing our gifts and stepping into our personal power, so that we can make a real difference in our own lives, a difference to our communities and a difference to the planet.

Chemical Composition

Although there are 118 elements shown on the Periodic Table of chemical elements, only 92 of them are naturally occurring. Of these, eight elements make up 98 per cent of the weight of the Earth's crust. Approximately three-quarters of the crust by weight is made of just two elements, oxygen and silicon. This is why the quartz family of crystals, made of silicon dioxide, is so abundant. The other six common elements occurring in the crust are aluminium, iron, calcium, sodium, potassium and magnesium. Most crystals are made of chemical compounds containing the most common elements, but a few – such as the metals gold, silver and copper – are single elements.

The chemical composition of crystals can be expressed as chemical formulae. For some crystals the formula is short and easy to remember: for example, the whole of the quartz family has the same basic chemical formula of SiO_2, which is silicon dioxide. The range of colours is due to various trace elements. Some common crystals have long and complex formulae, which you are unlikely to memorize. Although you may not remember a long chemical formula, provided you can decipher the symbols you will have some idea of what the crystal contains. It is worth becoming literate in the elements commonly found in crystals, as these can give you an insight into what the crystal's properties may be. For instance, haematite contains iron in its formula, Fe, which is a clue to its general strengthening properties and its traditional use for supporting the blood.

Most crystals are considered safe to handle, because even toxic elements are usually held in a stable and non-reactive form within a crystal, although this isn't the case for all crystals. If you are in any doubt about the toxicity of a crystal, do some careful research.

CAUTION: Never place crystals in your mouth or ingest them, however safe and non-toxic they may be. Keep crystals away from young children and pets, as they can be a choking hazard. Do not place crystals with possible toxicity in water. Levels of crystal toxicity must be put into context. Almost anything can become toxic if you are over-exposed to it. As the old adage states, "It is the dose that makes the poison." People have managed to poison themselves by eating quantities of carrots, apple seeds or green potatoes. Normal handling and use of most common crystals is extremely safe.

Table of Chemical Symbols

Symbol	Element	Points of interest and safety information	Example crystal
Al	Aluminium	Small amounts of aluminium are used by the body in the production of enzymes, although in larger doses aluminium can be toxic. The use of aluminium in cooking pots has been linked to Alzheimer's disease. The aluminium found in crystals is normally in a stable form, so the exposure to aluminium is minimal.	Sapphire: Al_2O_3
As	Arsenic	Arsenic is a well-known poison and is highly toxic. It was formerly used as a pigment, and arsenic in wallpapers and paints may have been the demise of some Victorians. Do not handle or use crystals containing arsenic.	Realgar: As_4S_4
B	Boron	Boron may be toxic if ingested at high levels, but in small amounts it helps build strong bones and is sometimes used as a supplement to treat arthritis and osteoporosis. Normal handling of boron containing crystals is safe.	Danburite: $CaB_2Si_2O_8$
Ba	Barium	The element barium is toxic, but it is stable and non-soluble in the crystal baryte, and handling baryte is not hazardous. You may be given a "barium meal" made of barium sulphate to drink before an X-ray of the digestive system.	Baryte: $BaSO_4$
Be	Beryllium	Beryllium is a toxic element, although in the beryl family of crystals it is stable and non-reactive, therefore it is safe to handle beryl crystals such as aquamarine, emerald and morganite.	Emerald: $Be_3Al_2(Si_6O_{18})$
C	Carbon	Humans are carbon-based life forms, and just under 20 per cent of our body mass is made of carbon, which is readily available through our diet. Carbon is often used for purification in water filters.	Diamond: C

Symbol	Element	Points of interest and safety information	Example crystal
Ca	Calcium	Calcium helps to form healthy bones and is used in other body processes too. We take in calcium through our diet and it is contained in dairy products and green leafy vegetables.	Calcite: $CaCO_3$
Cl	Chlorine	The element chlorine is a toxic gas at room temperature; however it forms half of the sodium chloride molecule, otherwise known as table salt. Salt is needed in the diet in small quantities as an electrolyte, to help regulate fluid balance in the body. Ingesting too much salt is harmful.	Halite: NaCl
Cr	Chromium	The body's metabolism uses tiny amounts of chromium. Chromium is toxic if ingested in larger quantities. The chromium content in ruby is stable, which means it is safe to handle.	Ruby: Al_2O_3(+Cr)
Cu	Copper	Copper is essential to life as a trace element. Many popular crystals contain copper, and it is responsible for giving these crystals their varying shades of greens to turquoises. Copper as a metal is a natural antimicrobial.	Malachite: $Cu_2CO_3(OH)_2$
F	Fluorine	The element fluorine is toxic; however fluoride is added to supplies of drinking water in some countries to strengthen tooth enamel. Water fluoridation is controversial. Fluoride is also a common additive in toothpaste. The fluorine in fluorite crystals is stable, so the crystal is safe to handle.	Fluorite: CaF_2
Fe	Iron	Iron-rich foods form part of a healthy diet, as iron is an important constituent of red blood cells, giving them their colour. It is a common element in crystals. Iron-rich crystals are often used in cases of anaemia, and historically were believed to staunch bleeding.	Haematite: Fe_2O_3

Symbol	Element	Points of interest and safety information	Example crystal
H	Hydrogen	Hydrogen is the lightest of all the elements and is explosive in the air in concentrations over 4 per cent. Bonded with oxygen, it forms the water molecule H_2O, which is essential for life. The human body is around 60 per cent water. Some crystals contain water in their formula; others contain hydroxide (OH).	Opal: SiO_2 n H_2O Larimar: $NaCa_2Si_3O_8(OH)$
Hg	Mercury	Mercury, or quicksilver, is a highly toxic element. Mercurius nitrate, historically used in hat-making, gave rise to the saying "as mad as a hatter", because mercury poisoning did send hat-makers mad. Cinnabar is an ore of mercury. If heated, it releases mercury vapour that condenses as liquid mercury. Do not handle cinnabar.	Cinnabar: HgS
K	Potassium	Potassium is essential for life, helping to regulate fluid balance, and is an important element for muscle and nerve signals. We get enough potassium through a healthy diet rich in fruits and vegetables.	Amazonite: $KalSi_3O_8$
Li	Lithium	Lithium compounds have been used to calm mania since the 19th century. Lithium is still used for bipolar disorder, but as a drug it can have some unpleasant side-effects. Lithium-containing crystals have gentle calming qualities.	Kunzite: $LiAlSi_2O_6$
Mg	Magnesium	Magnesium is an important element in the body and is used in many systems, including the nervous system, immune system, skeletal system and muscular system. Eating plenty of leafy greens is the best dietary source of magnesium.	Peridot: Mg_2SiO_4
Mn	Manganese	Manganese is a trace element that is important for brain function, the health of the nervous system and the production of some enzymes. You can get enough manganese by eating a healthy wholefood diet. Manganese is responsible for the colour of some pink crystals.	Rhodocrosite: $MnCO_3$
Na	Sodium	Sodium is the other half of the salt molecule NaCl and, as such, is important for the regulation of bodily fluids. Sodium is found in other common crystals, which often share an ability to clarify perception.	Sodalite: $Na_8(Al_6Si_6O_{24})Cl_2$

Symbol	Element	Points of interest and safety information	Example crystal
O	Oxygen	Oxygen is abundant on planet Earth. Oxygen in the air we breathe and the water we drink is essential for life. A large percentage of crystals contain oxygen in their chemical formula, including the whole of the quartz family with their basic formula of silicon dioxide.	Clear quartz: SiO_2
P	Phosphorous	Phosphorous as an element is highly reactive, but it is never found in nature as a free element. It is important for the formation of bones and teeth and plays a part in a wide range of metabolic functions, including the growth, repair and maintenance of tissues. We absorb plenty of phosphorous through a normal healthy diet. An excess of phosphorous in the body can be toxic.	Turquoise: $CuAl_6(PO_4)_4(OH)_8 \cdot 4H_2O$
Pb	Lead	Lead used to be a common ingredient in paint and fuel, but it has been removed because of its toxicity. Lead-containing crystals include cerussite, vanadinite and wulfenite. They should not be placed in water. Wash your hands after handling and keep them away from children.	Cerussite: $PbCO_3$
S	Sulphur	Sulphur is present in all living tissues and is used in many metabolic processes. It is abundantly available through a normal diet. Sulphur as a crystal is extremely soft and crumbles to dust easily, so handle it gently and don't expose it to water because it is soluble.	Pyrite: FeS_2
Sb	Antimony	Antimony is a toxic element that may be found in stibnite, which is antimony trisulphide. This can grow as attractive metallic-bladed crystals. It is a soft crystal, which was historically made into a paste as make-up, to darken eyelashes and eyebrows. Stibnite is best avoided.	Stibnite: Sb_2S_3

Symbol	Element	Points of interest and safety information	Example crystal
Si	Silicon	Silicon is abundant in the Earth's crust, second only to oxygen, which is why the quartz-family crystals made of silicon dioxide are so plentiful. It is non-toxic and is present as a trace element in the body, helping the formation of healthy nails, hair and skin. Silicon is hazardous to the lungs if breathed in as dust, potentially leading to the serious lung disease silicosis. Gem-cutters and carvers are at risk if they are not wearing respiratory protection.	Clear quartz: SiO_2
Sr	Strontium	Strontium is used in the body for healthy bone formation and helps to maintain bone density. It is sometimes used as a supplement for those with osteoporosis, but the safety and efficacy of this treatment are not proven. Strontium is available through a healthy varied diet.	Celestite: $SrSO_4$
Ti	Titanium	Titanium is a strong and lightweight metal. It doesn't corrode and is considered the most bio-compatible of all the metals. It is used to create high-quality, long-lasting joint replacements and dental implants.	Rutilated quartz: $SiO_2 + TiO_2$
Zn	Zinc	Zinc is used in the body by the immune system, for wound-healing, in enzymes and for other metabolic processes. It cannot be stored in the body, but you can get enough zinc by eating a varied wholefood diet.	Sphalerite: $(ZnFe)S$
Zr	Zirconium	Zirconium takes its name from zircon, which contains the element. There are traces of zirconium in the human body, but it isn't clear whether it has a biological function.	Zircon: $ZrSiO_4$

Mohs Scale of Hardness

Mohs Scale of Hardness is named after its creator, the mineralogist Friedrich Mohs, who developed it in 1812. It has been a test of mineral hardness ever since. Mohs selected ten crystals that varied in hardness and put them in order. The scale is simple, running from one for the softest mineral to ten for the hardest. It is not an even scale; the progression between hardness levels varies. Diamond, for example, at a hardness of ten, is much harder than corundum, at a hardness of nine.

The scratch test is based on everyday items that a 19th-century mineral collector might have to hand. It is a practical way to help identify rocks found in the field. It is only an approximate guide, as some crystals vary in hardness and fall between the levels on the scale. For greater accuracy, a range of hardness and half-numbers are used in the Crystal Directory (see pages 172–293); for example, jet is soft and ranges from 2.5 to 4 in hardness, and turquoise ranges between 5 and 6.

Mohs Scale of Hardness

Hardness level	Scratch test	Example crystals
1	Easily scratched by a fingernail	Talc
2	Scratched by a fingernail	Gypsum, selenite, halite, amber, seraphinite
3	Scratched by copper	Calcite, celestite, howlite
4	Easily scratched with a penknife	Fluorite, malachite, rhodocrosite
5	Barely scratched by a penknife	Larimar, lapis lazuli, moldavite
6	Scratched by a steel file	Obsidian, pyrite, labradorite, sunstone, amazonite
7	Will scratch window glass	Quartz family, peridot, tourmaline
8	Scratches glass easily	Beryl family, topaz
9	Will cut glass	Corundum – ruby, sapphire
10	Scratches everything else	Diamond

Scratching crystals in your collection as a means of identification is a last resort, as you would be making a mark on them; but if you use a scratch test, place the crystal on a non-slip surface, use firm pressure and carry the test out where it will be least visible. You might need a magnifying glass to see the scratch in harder crystals. Some crystals are quite brittle and break easily, which is not necessarily the same as being soft, so be careful with delicate-looking specimens. If you enjoy "rockhounding" (collecting rocks and minerals in the field) and want to check your finds, then hardness kits containing minerals you can use for testing are available. They don't normally contain a diamond, as this would make them too expensive.

Hardness information is useful for anyone interested in crystals as it gives an insight into how to store and handle them. Be mindful that harder stones can scratch softer ones. If you put all your crystals into one big bowl or bag and then rummage around, the soft ones will start to look sorry for themselves. Carrying soft stones in a pocket with loose change, or car keys, can easily scratch them and dull their shine.

Mineral hardness can provide a guide to the durability of crystals used in jewellery. Softer crystals are best reserved for occasional wear, whereas harder crystals can be worn every day. As a general rule, reserve crystal jewellery with a hardness under six for gentle occasional wear only. Mineral hardness is one reason that heirloom jewellery is usually made from gems of a hardness between eight and ten. These are much more likely to survive through the generations in good condition.

Mohs Scale provides an insight into the likely healing action of the crystal. Softer crystals tend to absorb energies and are typically good for detoxifying, whereas hard crystals tend to be better for directing and transmitting energy.

How Does Crystal Healing Work?

The simple answer is no one really knows for certain, but from experience it does. A scientific explanation may lie in the realm of quantum physics, which is an evolving branch of science with exciting implications for the field of healing in general, and crystal healing in particular.

Physicists have now proven that everything in the universe is made of energy. Once it was thought that an atom was the smallest particle in existence, but now we know that atoms contain protons, neutrons and electrons. Scientists then discovered that protons and neutrons are comprised of quarks and gluons. The further they go down the electron microscope, the more they discover that nothing is solid. Everything is made of energy in a constant state of movement and vibration.

Crystals, by definition, have an ordered lattice structure and may hold their structure over aeons of time. Because of their orderly nature, their energy field remains relatively stable and constant. It is this stability that has led to the use of crystals in industry. In contrast, a human being is an incredibly complex, ever-changing energy field. Our complexity makes it harder for us to maintain a healthy vibrational state. It is theorized that the benefits of crystal healing come from choosing a crystal with the precise energy required for health and introducing it to the human energy field, where it restores vibrational harmony through energy resonance.

Of course, people have been aware of the healing energy emanated by crystals for thousands of years. Quantum physics has put a possible scientific explanation forward for what were previously seen as purely spiritual or magical properties.

A less scientific, but more easily understood, analogy for the benefits of crystal healing is to liken the human body to an orchestra. When the instruments are tuned and the musicians are playing well, the sound is beautiful. If one instrument goes out of tune, or a musician loses their timing, the harmony is disrupted; if they continue to play out of tune or out of time, then the other musicians around them may become distracted and the whole sound of the orchestra may become discordant.

The body is, of course, much more complex than any orchestra. Like the orchestra, the systems of the body are interrelated and interdependent. The body works to achieve harmony between its various systems via a natural balancing process called "homeostasis". Most health issues begin with a small problem, which at first may be easy to ignore; however, if that is not corrected by the body's own healing processes, the issue can grow and become more entrenched. Once one body system falls out of harmony, a health issue may have a knock-on effect that can be experienced across other systems. Placing a carefully chosen crystal can act rather like a "tuning fork" and introduce the right "note" for the body to recalibrate itself and start the process of healing.

Apart from the effect of the crystalline lattice on vibration, crystals have a colour, and each colour has a specific vibrational frequency. Colour healing is a discipline that is becoming more accepted and mainstream in its application. Some institutions, such as hospitals and schools, are using colour in their decor to create a more welcoming or calming atmosphere, and restaurants have long been aware of the effect of colour on the length of time their diners want to spend at their tables. Crystals are a beautiful way to engage with colour therapy. Each crystal can be seen as carrying a frequency of light in a stable and easy-to-use form. Clear crystals, such as clear quartz, carry the frequency of white light, which can be split by a prism into the colour rays. As such, these crystals are considered to be master healers.

Many crystals contain minerals that are needed for the healthy functioning of the human body. Historically some cultures ground crystals to a powder, to ingest them as medicines. This is not safe and crystals shouldn't be taken internally. However, many healers believe that the mineral content of the crystals can work energetically to support the body in utilizing the necessary minerals from the diet; so, for example, if someone has osteoporosis, they might want to work with crystals containing calcium and magnesium, as these minerals support bone health.

Many people have a more esoteric belief in the efficacy of crystals. Just as some tribal cultures regard crystals as beings in their own right, many modern healers and spiritual seekers feel the same. Some crystals seem to have a distinctive personality, and those who are more intuitive may begin to receive messages and guidance from them. Many people find that treating crystals as allies – rather than as inanimate healing tools – leads to a richer and more personal experience of the crystal kingdom.

Many crystals are truly ancient, and formed long ago. Even the longest human life is short compared to a crystal, which may be millions, or even billions, of years old, and yet we each have an eternal spirit. Holding a crystal may stir the sense of eternity within you. Sometimes crystals awaken memories of other lifetimes, and a lot of people who are drawn to crystals believe that they have done healing with them before. For these people, meeting the crystals and finding out about them is more like a remembrance and a reconnection. You may wonder at times whether you chose the crystals or whether they chose you.

COLOURS AND VIBRATIONAL FREQUENCY

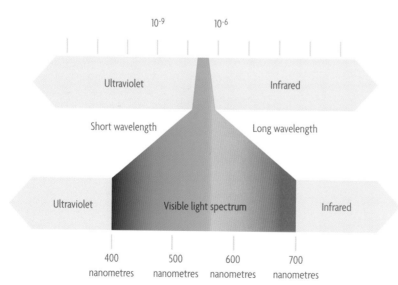

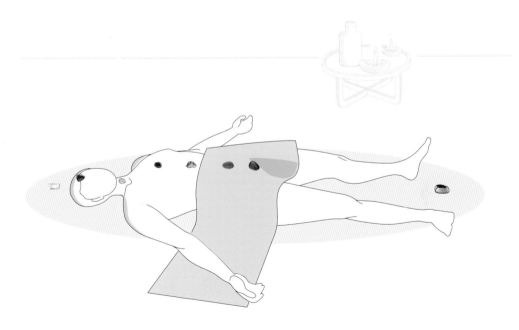

2
ENERGY
SAFETY

Grounding

Getting "grounded" is the first and most important step you need to take to ensure your energy is stable and secure enough to tune into, and work with, crystals. It describes the way your personal energy is connected to the energy of the Earth. Making physical or energetic contact with the ground is often referred to as "earthing" and is valuable for everyone.

We evolved to be connected to the Earth's energy, and in traditional cultures this is not an issue. When much of life is spent outdoors, with the feet making direct contact with the Earth, being grounded is automatic. The more sophisticated our lives have become, the more divorced we are from this natural connection. We increasingly live indoors and, when we venture out, we usually wear shoes with rubber or synthetic soles that insulate us from the ground. Ask yourself, "When was the last time I walked barefoot on the ground outdoors?"

Modern technology exposes us to electromagnetic fields (EMFs) and radio frequencies (RFs) that our ancestors never encountered. Regular use of mobile phones and personal computers affects our energy field. Staying earthed helps us discharge harmlessly into the ground the energy that we absorb from these devices.

While earthing is healthy for everyone, becoming more deeply grounded is important for anyone who is opening spiritually. Without deep grounding roots, the expansion of consciousness that comes with spiritual awakening can be destabilizing. Think of your grounding as the firm foundation upon which your spiritual development builds.

Some people are naturally blessed with strong grounding. If you are even-tempered, practical, level-headed, unflappable in a crisis and feel secure most of the time, then chances are you are one of these people. If, on the other hand, you frequently feel anxious or easily upset, have volatile moods and feel insecure, then your grounding is likely to be an issue. Being clumsy, dropping things or tripping up can be a sign that you have lost your grounding. If you frequently get distracted and people describe you as being "away with the fairies", then you are almost certainly ungrounded. Most people fall somewhere in between the two extremes and are sometimes grounded, sometimes not.

You can become aware of your grounded state and are likely to feel steadier on your feet and sturdier. Strong grounding may be sensed as tingling or warmth in the soles of your feet, or a feeling of being firmly "planted".

For an analogy of how grounding can support your spiritual development, think of a tree. A tree that grows tall but only puts down shallow roots is likely to be blown over. A tree that puts down deep roots can grow tall and withstand stormy weather.

Grounding with Crystals

There are plenty of crystals that can help you establish and maintain a grounded connection with the Earth. As a general guide, black, brown and red stones will have some grounding properties. Crystals containing metals such as iron or lead in their chemical composition will also be grounding. These crystals feel heavy for their size, and their extra weight can be reassuring and provide the sense of security that comes with groundedness.

One of the most accessible and popular grounding crystals is haematite, which contains iron. The Earth is believed to have a high proportion of iron at her core, so iron-rich crystals like haematite can help you "drop anchor" and connect deeply into the Earth.

Big isn't always better in the world of crystals. However, large grounding stones can be a worthwhile investment if you tend to be ungrounded. Have a few smaller grounding stones you can carry around with you too.

Other good grounding crystals include black tourmaline, red jasper, garnet, smoky quartz, tiger's eye and obsidian. Tiger iron can be useful because it combines three grounding stones in one, as it is made of haematite, red jasper and tiger's eye. This is sometimes sold under its alternative trade name of "mugglestone".

If you feel ungrounded, carry grounding crystals in your pockets. Trouser pockets are preferable, because they place the crystal close to your base chakra, which is the chakra, or energy centre, that connects you most naturally with the Earth.

When you are seated you can sit on a grounding stone, but choose a smooth one! You can also place a grounding stone between your feet or under your chair.

A lot of people lose their grounding when they lie down and feel more vulnerable at night. If this is the case for you, try a large grounding stone placed at the foot end of the bed.

Anchoring Your Energy with Haematite

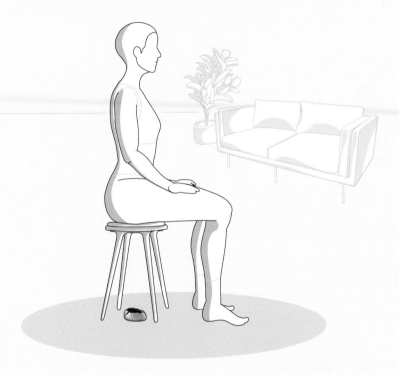

1. Sit with your back upright. If you only have one piece of haematite, place it directly under your chair in line with your base chakra (see page 86). If you have several pieces, you can sit on another piece.

2. Close your eyes and take a few deep breaths. Focus your attention on the base of your spine. Imagine an energy cord extending downward from your coccyx, like a big tap root. You may feel some tingling at your base chakra as you do this. See the cord of energy passing down through the layers of the Earth and being drawn magnetically toward the iron at her core.

3. Feel the connection to the Earth's iron core strengthening you, helping you to feel secure and stable. You can see the anchoring cord of light is flexible and you can move freely, but you stay firmly anchored to the planet.

4. Once you sense your connection is established, take a few deep breaths and open your eyes. If you need a reminder to stay grounded, keep a piece of haematite with you as you go through your day.

A Grounding Layout

This layout is useful if you feel ungrounded and would like to relax and let the crystals do the work. You will need four grounding stones. If you have four matching crystals that's ideal, but use whatever you have.

1. You will be lying down for this exercise. Lie down, note where your feet reach to and then place one grounding stone about 30cm (12in) away, in alignment with your feet. This stimulates an energy centre called the Earth star, which helps you to stay grounded.

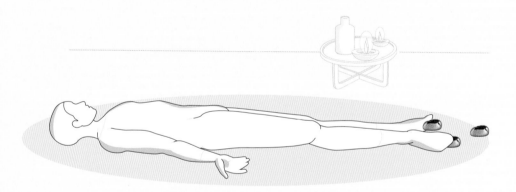

2. Now put a grounding stone beneath the sole of each foot.

3. Lie down again and place the last grounding stone between your legs at the top of your thighs.

4. Relax and notice any shifts in your energy, paying particular attention to the soles of your feet. Ten minutes in this layout should be plenty, but if you are enjoying it you can rest there longer.

Centring

Centring gathers your energy and brings your awareness into the moment. Once you are centred you feel more present, calmer and better able to deal with whatever you need to focus on. You centre your energy by drawing your awareness down into your body, focusing your energy in the lower belly, the solar plexus (see page 90) or the heart. Which centre you choose is up to you. Most people will find they have a preference.

Centring at the Tan Tien

In martial arts such as Tai Chi and Chi Kung, practitioners centre their energy in the lower belly, about three fingers' width below the naval, using an energy centre called the Tan Tien. This centre can be thought of as an energy reservoir with the capacity to store power to keep you feeling healthy and vital. It is the centre of gravity for the body when standing, and for this reason centring here can make you feel physically stronger and more stable. If you have any issues with grounding, centring at the Tan Tien will probably help.

In Chinese Traditional Medicine this energy centre is called a "cinnabar field". The Chinese prized cinnabar for its beautiful red colour, although as cinnabar is a toxic crystal containing mercury, it is much safer to use another strengthening red crystal.

1. Choose a red crystal such as red jasper, garnet or ruby. Hold it and stand upright with your feet hip-width apart, let your shoulders drop and relax your belly.

2. Take a few deep breaths and bring your attention to your Tan Tien, feeling your energy dropping into this part of your body.

3. Hold your chosen crystal to your lower belly. As you pay attention to the area of your Tan Tien you may become aware of warmth, or imagine a glowing light there. Spending a few minutes a day on this exercise is enough to make a tangible difference to your physical vitality.

Centring at the Solar Plexus

The solar plexus is situated above your naval and below your breastbone.
A complex system of radiating nerves is centred here, which is what the
term "plexus" refers to. This is the location of your solar plexus chakra, which
processes energy and supports your sense of personal power and your will.

1. Choose a golden crystal such as pyrite, citrine or rutilated quartz. Hold the crystal and stand or sit upright.

2. Take a few deep breaths. Relax your shoulders and bring your attention to your solar plexus. Breathe into your solar plexus and hold your crystal over it.

3. Visualize, or imagine, a glowing ball of energy gathering here, golden and shining like the Sun. You may feel the area growing warmer. Spending a few minutes a day centring at your solar plexus can improve your energy levels, empower you and build your resolve.

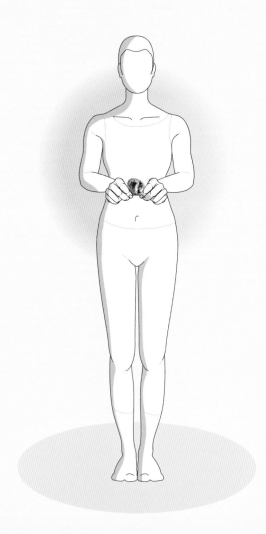

Centring at the Heart

Centring at the heart is a good choice for healers and those working in the caring professions, as it encourages compassion. The heart is the meeting point in the chakra system between the physical lower chakras and the spiritual higher chakras and, as such, it is a place of balance and equilibrium. For healers, centring at the heart will help the healing energy to flow. The stream of healing energy from the universe and the nurturing energy from the Earth can be brought to meet at the heart, then flow through the arms and out to the recipient through the palm chakras.

1. Choose a green crystal such as aventurine or a pink crystal such as rose quartz. Hold your chosen crystal and stand or sit upright.

2. Take a few deep breaths. Bring your attention to your heart centre in the middle of your chest. Focus on your breathing in this area as you hold your crystal to the heart chakra. You may feel warmth or sense a glowing pink or green energy as you centre here. By centring at the heart for a few minutes a day you may find you become less judgemental and more understanding.

Protection

We live in a world of duality, where everything has its equal and opposite. There are positive and negative energies, and everyone has a light side and a shadow side. It is exciting when you begin to sense unseen energies, but to imagine that everything unseen is good for you would be naive. Working with crystals can heighten your awareness of the subtle realms, so it is advisable to protect your energy.

Developing sensitivity to energy is helpful. You may notice unpleasant or heavy energies more quickly and be better able to distinguish between relationships, groups and places that are supportive and those that are draining or unhealthy.

Shielding your energy is important for anyone who works with other people, especially those in jobs where the clients are unwell or want to offload their troubles. It is especially important for healers and therapists to shield themselves, as a large part of healing is about encouraging the other person to release energies that have been weighing them down. Therapists who don't protect their energy often become depressed and unwell because they absorb too much from their clients.

You won't necessarily know when protection would come in useful, so get into the habit of doing it after your grounding and centring each morning as a simple routine, in the same way that you brush your teeth and get dressed. Shielding your energy using crystals is a lovely thing to do for yourself and takes very little time. In this way your shield is there, whatever the day has in store for you.

Almost any crystal can be used to surround your energy field as a shield. Each crystalline shield feels different, so try out a few crystals to find one that you like, or vary your crystal shield according to your intuition. The options are as varied as the crystals themselves.

You could visualize a glossy black obsidian shell around your aura or energy field. Any difficult energies simply slide off the surface and down into the earth, where they can be recycled, a bit like composting them.

Labradorite can become a magical cloak of coloured light for your aura. When you want to get on with things without interruption, you can picture your cloak as a nondescript grey. When you want to be noticed, it can shine with shifting colours of bright blues, golds and greens.

Your shield could be made from thousands of brightly faceted gemstones, which break up heavy energies with their sparkling rays of light. You are not limited by your finances when you visualize, so you might choose to surround your aura with expensive jewels, such as sapphires, diamonds, emeralds or rubies.

If you are going through a particularly tough time and it feels like you are under siege, or attracting a lot of negative energy, then black tourmaline is strongly protective. Alternatively, use iron pyrite to visualize a suit of shining golden armour for yourself, if you feel you need to "go into battle".

Your crystalline protection can be strengthened by carrying the matching crystal with you, or by wearing it as jewellery. This helps to keep your shield firmly in place without you needing to place any more attention on it.

On Guidance and Keeping a Development Journal

Using crystals may open you to spiritual guidance, which can come in a variety of ways. Most guidance is quiet and subtle. The "small still voice" is the way that God spoke to Elijah in the Bible and is how you may receive guidance. The small still voice within you is quiet, and you need to allow your mind to be peaceful to hear it, otherwise it will be drowned out by your own mental chatter. Whether you believe this is the voice of God, your guardian angel, a Spirit Guide or your own Higher Self, you should take note of the quality of the guidance. True spiritual guidance has a wise, reassuring and supportive quality. It may sound like a quieter version of your own voice, but the quality of the guidance will be wiser than your conscious mind would normally supply.

You may receive guidance images in your third eye or brow chakra (see page 96), and visions during meditation, visualizations and peaceful reverie. Sometimes the images are symbolic and will need decoding.

You may also receive messages through your dreams. While you sleep your conscious mind is resting and it can be easier for guidance to get through. Write down dreams that seem more vivid or meaningful than usual. Dream guidance is often symbolic.

Many people start to notice more synchronicity in their lives when they use crystals. Synchronicity is used to describe meaningful coincidences. If guidance is particularly significant, then the same message may come through in a variety of ways. Perhaps you randomly open a book at a page containing the message, then see significant words or images on a lorry, then switch on the television just as the topic is featured.

You may simply have an "inner knowing", which is hard to explain but may be the most reliable guidance of all. Pay attention to your gut instincts, hunches and intuitions. You may find that your on-board guidance system can save you from making expensive mistakes and unwise choices.

Record the guidance you receive in a journal. Often guidance will come in fragments and you won't receive the whole message in one go. It isn't until you have more pieces that you can understand its meaning. It can feel as if you are on a spiritual treasure hunt. Keeping a journal gives you somewhere safe to note your insights, helps you to track your spiritual development and can be interesting to look back on. You can record your impressions of your crystals and your experiences with them too.

If you experience an inner voice that is unpleasant – if it is shouting, scolding or haranguing you – then this is not a voice of spiritual guidance. Be discerning. We all have an inner critic that likes to bring us down. You don't need to pay attention to it.

Considerations When Using Crystals for Healing

Crystals can work through clothing. Crystalline energy easily penetrates thin layers of clothing, so there is no need to take all your clothes off for a crystal healing. You can place crystals against bare skin for self-treatment if you prefer, but if you go to a professional crystal healer, they will usually only ask you to remove bulky outer clothing, such as coats and heavy sweaters and your shoes.

Try to choose a time when you will not be disturbed, and turn off your mobile phone. Crystals can send you into a pleasant state of altered consciousness and being interrupted can make you jump and feels unpleasant, rather like being woken suddenly from a deep sleep.

Always have a grounding stone (see page 38) close to hand when you meditate or do healing with crystals. Crystals can make you feel like you have been out among the stars or on a different plane of existence, and you may need the grounding stone to "bring you back to Earth" at the end of your session. For the same reason, don't jump straight up and try to get back to normal activities. Give yourself a few minutes to come round properly; have a drink of water. You can use this time to make any notes in your journal.

Crystals can provoke a strong reaction, and sometimes they feel uncomfortable when placed. The reaction varies from a feeling of pressure or weight that is out of proportion to the size of the stone, to pain. If you can cope, try to relax and breathe deeply, as this is often a sign that the crystal is hard at work. The discomfort will usually ease within a few minutes. If you really dislike the sensation, then remove the crystal. You can try the same stone again later or use a different crystal.

Crystals may provoke a healing crisis. Although the name sounds scary, a healing crisis is normally a positive sign that you are having a detox. Once the symptoms have settled, you will usually feel better than you did beforehand. A "crisis" can be caused when a lot of old, stagnant or unhealthy energy is shifted in one session. Symptoms of a healing crisis relate to the ways in which the body clears itself of unhelpful energies as quickly as possible. These may include feeling cold and shivery, being tearful, having loose or smelly bowel movements, needing to urinate frequently, being flatulent or feeling exhausted. If you experience a healing crisis, then rest and recuperate, stay warm and drink plenty of fluids, especially water, to help flush the old energies out of your system. Healing-crisis symptoms normally ease off within 24–48 hours. If they are more prolonged or if you are worried about your symptoms, seek medical attention, as it is possible that you have a more physical ailment.

As crystals can help you release stagnant and unhealthy energies from your system, it is best not to do a crystal healing on your bed. You may release unpleasant energies, which then sink into your mattress, where you will have to sleep amid them. A better solution is to lie on a yoga mat on the floor. If you feel you have had a detox, then it is worth cleansing your mattress with sound, washing your bedding and airing quilts and pillowcases, as the body often clears out old energies while you are sleeping.

3
TUNING
INTO
CRYSTALS

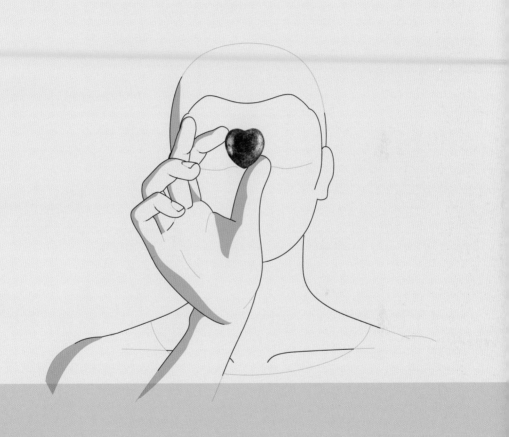

Choosing Your Crystals

How do you know which is the best crystal for you to work with? The Crystal Directory (see pages 172–293) is a guide, but the crystal you need is not always the one that logic would point to. Choosing a crystal is an intuitive process.

There are several ways to choose crystals and it is a good idea to try them and find out which ones you like best. First, you need to form a clear intention. Ask yourself what you would like the crystal to help you with. Possible intentions include:

- To boost my confidence
- To help me stay grounded
- To calm my nerves
- To help me focus
- To ease discomfort in [area] of my body
- To boost my self-esteem
- To help me meditate
- To open my heart to love
- To support my energy levels

If you don't have a specific reason for choosing a crystal, but just like to carry one with you, you can set the intention that you will choose the best crystal for today. Sometimes a few crystals may work well in combination for you, and you could be drawn to several for this reason.

You can also use the choosing methods to pick crystals for another person. For example, if you want to buy a crystal gift for a friend, simply change your intention to choosing the best crystal for them, and hold an image of your friend in your mind's eye.

Sight

Crystals are attractive and looking at them is a pleasure. Once you have formed your intention, gaze across the crystals and see which one your eye is most taken with. Some people even see the right crystal seeming to glow a little. If you wear spectacles, experiment by choosing with your glasses on and then off. Some spectacle-wearers get clearer results when their vision is blurred.

Choosing by sight is an easy method, but the beautiful appearance of the crystals can be distracting. If you find you always pick the most attractive stones, try some of the other methods, as you may be missing out on the help of less showy crystals in your collection.

Intuition

Sometimes the name of the crystal you need simply pops into your mind, or you get an image of it. This is your intuition at work. On a higher level you already know which crystal would be good for you right now. Intuition tends to come in when you are not trying too hard – often when you are feeling relaxed and haven't really been thinking of anything much. You may even find that you dream of the crystal you need to work with.

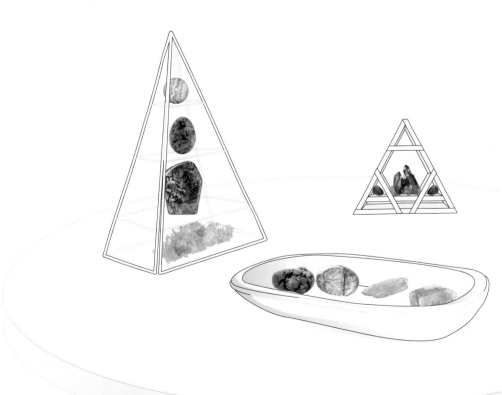

Hand Scanning

Crystals have energy fields. When you set a clear intention and pass your hand across a crystal that can assist you, there will be a subtle response from the crystal. Some people prefer to close their eyes with this method, so they can focus on the sensations in their hands without visual distraction. The left hand is regarded as the more receptive hand and is often more sensitive, but try using your right hand too and find out which one works best for you.

First, wake up the energy in your hands. Give your hands a wash, or a shake, to clear them of any residual energies. Next rub them briskly together for a minute or so, until they feel warm and tingly. Now set your intention and pass your hand slowly across your crystals, holding it 2.5cm (1in) or so above them. Notice any sensations in your palm and fingertips. Some crystal energies may feel cool, some warm, and others might feel like they are pulling your hand magnetically toward them. It can help with the final selection if you pick out the crystals you got the most response from and spread them out. Pass your hand over them again. Which crystal energy attracts you the most?

Lucky Dip

A lucky dip is an easy way to engage the power of synchronicity. Synchronicity describes the way that meaningful things happen by seeming coincidence. It is one way that spiritual guidance can often come to us. Place your crystals into a cloth bag, focus on your intention and then put your hand in the bag and pull a crystal out.

You will need to use crystals that are robust enough for this treatment. Soft and delicate crystals could be damaged by being placed in a bag with other crystals. The lucky-dip method works best with tumblestones (see page 167) of similar size, so that you don't recognize the crystals by their shape, size or texture, which could influence your choice.

Crystal Cards

This is another quick and easy way to engage synchronicity. Crystal oracle cards are available in several different styles, or you can even make your own. Choose a deck of crystal cards that you are attracted to. Look through them and remove those that refer to crystals you don't yet have in your collection. Now set your intention, give the cards a good shuffle and fan them out face-down in front of you. Your eye may be drawn to the card you need, or you can scan across them all with your hand, to feel which card you are drawn to. Pick the card and look at the crystal picture, then go and pick the corresponding crystal to work with. Looking at the oracle reading may give you some useful insights too.

If you would like to make your own crystal cards, either cut some thin card to size or buy packs of plain postcards. Write the name of each type of crystal in your collection on one side of the card. You can decorate the card by photographing the crystal, or draw or paint your crystal. You can add some key words to help you learn about the crystal, and useful information such as its hardness or chemical formula. Leave the backs plain, or decorate them all with the same image, so that you can't tell which card is which when you fan them out to make your selection.

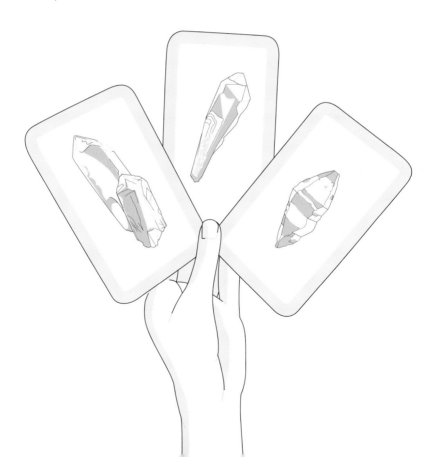

Pendulum Dowsing

Dowsing can be a fast and accurate way to choose your crystals, but you'll need to learn the art of pendulum dowsing first. A pendulum can be any weight on a chain or string. Crystal pendulums are available in a variety of types. The most versatile is clear quartz, but other members of the quartz family, such as rose quartz or amethyst, are also popular choices. The size of your pendulum isn't too important, but it should feel comfortable for you to use. Some people prefer delicate pendulums; others like the weight of a heavy pendulum. Choose a pendulum that you like the look and feel of.

A pendulum is a way of amplifying small muscle movements in your arm and hand, so that they become visible. The pendulum doesn't magically move itself; you are moving it. These small movements are a subtle way that your intuitive self can communicate with you. Some call this aspect their Higher Self, as it is eternally peaceful and unaffected by life's dramas.

First, make sure you have prepared your energy (see pages 36–45), as your dowsing is likely to be wildly inaccurate if you are not grounded and centred. Now hold the pendulum by the chain between the thumb and forefinger of your dominant hand. Hold it in front of you at a comfortable height so that you can see it, but not so high that you are making your arm uncomfortable – your arm should feel relaxed.

Dowsing can give you a positive "yes" response or a negative "no" response. Begin by asking a question that should give a "yes" response. For example, you could ask whether you like your favourite food. Asking the question in your head or out loud shouldn't make any difference. Watch your pendulum for a response. It may start to swing backward and forward or from side to side, or perhaps it moves in circles, clockwise or anticlockwise. Different people get different pendulum swings. If it doesn't move at all, or if the movement is tiny, relax your arm and then ask your question again. Keep asking questions to which there is "yes" response until you are happy that you recognize the way your pendulum swings when it is answering affirmatively.

Now ask a "no" question. For example, you could ask whether you like a food that you detest. Watch the way your pendulum responds. It should start to swing in a different way from your "yes" response.

For most people, "yes" and "no" swings remain the same, whichever pendulum they pick up; but a small percentage of people find that their swings change with different pendulums. It is easy to check by asking a "yes" and a "no" question, if you swap to a different pendulum.

Once you have established two different swings you are ready to choose a crystal by pendulum dowsing. Set your intention for choosing a crystal, then put your crystal into a gentle motion that is neither your "yes" nor your "no" swing – this is a neutral swing for you. It is useful to have a neutral swing, as it is easier for your pendulum to respond when gently moving rather than from a still position.

Either move your pendulum slowly over your crystals and wait for the swing change to a "yes" over the most positive choice, or gaze at the crystals and let your eyes travel slowly across them; your pendulum will change its swing to your "yes" when you are looking at the best choice of crystal. Similarly, you can pass your free hand across the crystals and wait for the pendulum to change its swing. If you have several crystals close together, you may need to fine-tune your selection by touching or pointing at individual crystals until you get a positive swing.

Pendulum dowsing can take a while to perfect. If your pendulum is only making small movements, roll your shoulders and relax your arm. Muscular tension is the main cause of small pendulum swings. Try holding your pendulum chain at a different point. Some people dowse better with a short chain, while others need a longer one. Experiment to find the optimum length for you. A different grip on your pendulum may help. Try holding it with the chain draped over your outstretched index finger and held securely between your thumb and middle finger.

Dowsing a List
Set your intention. Write down a list of the crystals you are considering using and then put your pendulum into its neutral swing. Run your finger down the list slowly and you will get a "yes" response when you reach the most appropriate crystal.

Dowsing an Arc
Dowsing an arc is an alternative to dowsing a list. Arcs are fan-shaped segmented charts. In each segment you can write the name of a crystal in your collection. Set your intention and then hold your pendulum over the arc. Set it swinging straight back and forth over the centre of the arc. Allow the pendulum to continue to swing as it moves toward the appropriate crystal. You'll sense when the pendulum has settled its swing over one crystal. If the segments in the arc are small, then you can place your finger on the individual crystal name and check, "Is it this one?" You'll get a "yes" swing for the correct crystal.

Kinesiology

Kinesiology, or muscle-testing, can be a fun way to choose a crystal using feedback from your own body. You will need someone to help you. A positive crystal energy will make your muscles test stronger, and an unhelpful crystal will make them test weaker.

First, you need to set up a baseline reading, so that your tester can feel how your muscle reacts without a crystal. Remove any crystal jewellery before you begin, as it can confuse your results. Put your arm out in front of you, holding it level with your shoulder. Alternatively, hold it out to the side, if that is more comfortable. Your helper needs to place two or three fingers on the top of your forearm just above your wrist. They should ask you to "resist" and then gently press down on your arm. How easily your arm moves gives a baseline.

Now choose a crystal and hold it in your other hand. Ask your helper to test your arm again, asking you to "resist" before pressing gently down. If your arm falls away more easily when you are holding the crystal, then that is an unhelpful energy for you at the moment. If your arm feels firmer, the crystal is strengthening and is helpful for you. You can close your eyes and let your helper choose a crystal for you, placing it in your hand. This way you know that you are not influencing your strong and weak responses according to your expectations.

If a few crystals test strong for you, then try them in combination. Sometimes their combined energies are even stronger; sometimes they will test weaker and need to be used individually, in which case work with whichever crystal tested strongest.

Muscle-testing is a great way to check whether your jewellery is supportive and whether the combination of rings, bracelets, earrings or necklaces you wish to wear will be strengthening for you.

Kinesiology can take some practice. If your arm is testing weak for everything, it is possible your helper is applying too much pressure. This isn't a test of whether you work out at the gym. It is also possible that your arm muscles are tired. Rest your arm between tests. Having a sip of water between each test can also help. If you decide to change arm, run through the baseline muscle-testing again.

Kinesiology can be useful if you want to set a personal goal or pursue an ambition. Write down your intention and make sure the wording is clear and positive. Ask your partner to test your arm while you state your goal aloud. Note how your arm feels. Now repeat your statement while holding your chosen crystal and notice whether your arm feels stronger or weaker. Keep testing using different crystals, singly or in combination, until your arm feels really strong. You may also notice your voice sounds more confident when you have chosen the right crystals. Holding these crystals on a daily basis while you focus on your intention can support you in achieving your goal.

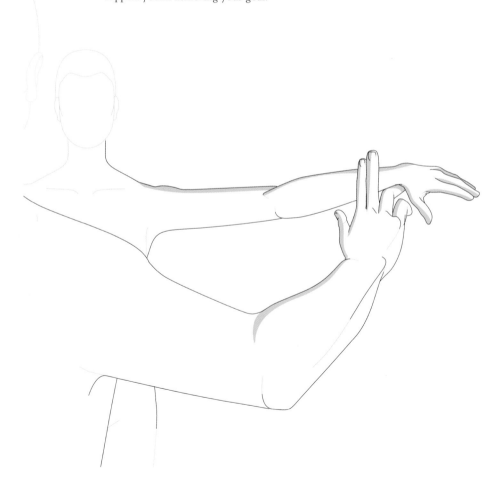

Attuning to a Crystal

Although you can look up the properties of your crystal in the Crystal Directory (see pages 172–293), the relationship between you and your crystal is unique. By attuning to your crystal, you open yourself on a more personal level to the healing and wisdom it contains. There is the potential for the crystal to become a true ally for your healing and spiritual development.

To find out what general effect the crystal has on you, simply keep your cleansed crystal (see page 66) close by and carry it around for a few days. Notice whether you feel any different in its presence. If the stone isn't too delicate or too spiky, you could pop it under your pillow and notice any changes to your dreams or sleep pattern. Remove the crystal from your bedroom if you find it is keeping you awake!

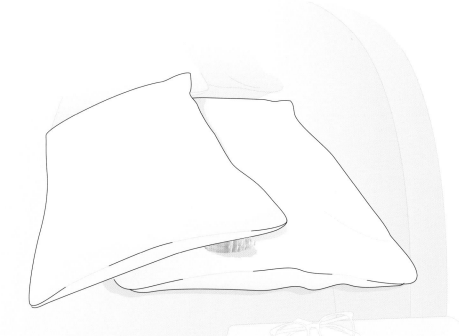

A Simple Crystal Attunement

1. Examine your cleansed crystal visually (see page 66). Look at it from all angles. Appreciate the colour and the way the light plays on it. Notice any patterns or crevices.

2. Now hold it in your hands and notice the weight of it, feel its shape. Run your fingers over the surface: is it smooth or rough?

3. Place it in the palm of your hand. Can you sense the energy of the crystal? Try it in the other hand. Does it feel the same or different? Hold it in the hand that feels most sensitive to the crystal.

4. Imagine you are sending a greeting to the crystal. In your mind say, "Hello". Invite the crystal's energy to merge with your own. You may sense tingling or warmth starting to travel into your hand and arm. Imagine the crystal's energy flowing into your bloodstream and being carried through your body in your blood.

5. Notice your body's reaction to the crystal. Where are you responding most strongly to the crystal? It may be an area where you feel tension or have health issues. You may want to hold the crystal there. Relax and imagine you can breathe into that area.

6. When you have finished, hold the crystal in your hand and ask whether it has a message for you. You may get a message in words, see a picture or have a feeling.

7. Say, "Thank you" to the crystal before you put it down. Make a note in your journal of everything that you experienced.

A Visit to the Crystal Temple

If you would like to meet your crystal on a deeper level, you can attune to it in the Crystal Temple.

1. Start by examining your cleansed crystal (see page 66) and familiarizing yourself with it.

2. Now close your eyes and take a few deep breaths. Visualize standing in a beautiful garden filled with fragrant flowers. You walk along the path and are drawn to pick one perfect flower. You carry it in your hand as you walk toward the centre of the garden, where you have glimpsed the white-domed roof of a temple.

3. The path opens out and the Crystal Temple stands ahead of you, up a short flight of steps. It is circular and made entirely of white crystal, which is glowing with a gentle light. You climb the steps and enter barefoot through the Temple door. The floor feels cool and smooth beneath your feet. The air inside the Temple is fresh. You see there is an altar ahead of you, with a lit candle upon it.

4. As you approach you are delighted to see your own crystal standing on the altar, looking larger and more beautiful than ever. It is shining with light. As you stand before the altar, your crystal shines more brightly and its light expands to surround you. Breathe in its radiant energy. Notice how you feel. You are aware that your crystal wishes to communicate with you. Listen to what it has to say.

5. Once you have finished communicating with your crystal, you place the flower on the altar as an offering of thanks before leaving the Temple.

6. Outside, you step back down into the garden and contemplate all you have learned and experienced.

7. When you are ready, let the images fade. Take a few deep breaths and open your eyes. Look again at your cleansed crystal, knowing you have made a deeper connection.

8. Write up your experience in your journal.

4

CARING FOR YOUR CRYSTALS

Cleansing Crystals

Your crystals need cleansing. Most crystals can hold on to stagnant or unpleasant energies – this is one of the ways they do their healing, by lifting away or absorbing heavy energies, leaving us feeling lighter.

Once you have handled crystals for a while you'll start to notice when crystals feel unclean. A crystal may feel sticky or heavy to the touch. It might look dull or less colourful than usual. This is not the same as being physically dirty, although – like anything else – crystals can get dirty and may need physical cleaning.

As a general guide, you should cleanse all your crystals when you first purchase them and then whenever you have used them. Crystals placed around your home also need regular cleansing. Some of the cleansing methods listed below have the advantage of being good ways to do space-clearing, which means they can cleanse and purify the energy in your home too.

Water

Most crystals can be cleansed in water, which is a cheap and convenient method. Washing your crystals has the advantage of physically cleaning them at the same time. Run a basin of warm water and, if your crystals are physically dirty, add a mild detergent. Give them a rinse in clean water.

Washing crystals under a running tap gives them a quick cleanse. If you have a lot of crystals to wash, you can place them in a plastic sieve or a laundry net bag. Only use this method to wash harder, more robust crystals because delicate or softer stones need more careful handing.

To give your crystals a treat, wash them in living waters, such as a clear stream, a waterfall or flowing spring water. Your crystals will love the experience and feel fresher for it.

A lot of people recommend cleansing crystals in salt water, either by dissolving salt in a bowl of water or by taking crystals to the sea. Salt is an ancient purifier, but it is potentially corrosive and can dull the surface lustre of some crystals. Salt water may also leave deposits on the surface of your crystals as it dries or crystallizes in crevices. If you use salt water, always follow with a thorough rinse in fresh water.

Some crystals may be damaged by water. The most common example is selenite, particularly the form called satin spar, which may fall apart lengthways along its crystalline structure if soaked. Iron-rich crystals such as raw haematite can rust, if left damp. If you must wash a water-sensitive crystal because it has got physically dirty, then expose it to the water for the shortest possible time, and dry it immediately afterwards with a soft towel to minimize the risk.

Salt lamps are carved from Himalayan rock salt and are lit by a bulb. They can start to look crusty and dull over time. A very quick wash and an immediate polish dry is a way to get the shine back. Be aware that every time you do this you are washing away a little more of your salt lamp. You must remove the electrical fitting before exposing your salt lamp to water.

Smoke

Purifying using sacred smoke has a long history, which continues to the present day. Many churches and temples purify using incense, and burning sacred herbs is a tradition across many tribal cultures. Cleansing your crystals with smoke can become a lovely ritual and is an easy way to cleanse a larger collection. Be aware of fire safety, and avoid using smoke if anyone in the household has breathing issues.

Incense

The best incense for cleansing crystals is solid incense. Ready-prepared blends made of tree resins and herbs can be purchased. Frankincense and myrrh have a long history – the Three Wise Men brought the infant Jesus gifts of gold, frankincense and myrrh. It is interesting that two out of three of their gifts were resins used for spiritual purification.

To burn solid incense you need a fireproof holder. Traditional censers are made from brass. To protect your furniture, you can place a heatproof mat underneath the censer. Ensure there is nothing flammable nearby that could cause a fire hazard. Burning incense must be placed safely out of reach of children and pets. Do not leave it burning unattended.

Solid incense is burned on a charcoal disc. These are available in rolls of ten and are stocked by New Age shops and ecclesiastical suppliers. Do not hold the disc between your fingers to light it; instead get a firm grip using small tongs, such as the ones sold for squeezing teabags. Light the disc from underneath using a long match or a lighter flame. Once it is lit, place it on the censer with the shallow cup uppermost. Be patient; allow the sparkling line of fire to move across the whole disc, and the disc to start glowing red.

Once the charcoal is hot, you can put a small spoonful of your solid incense into the little cup. You'll see the incense begin to melt and fragrant smoke will start to rise. At this point you can hold your crystals in the smoke to cleanse them. If you have a lot of crystals to cleanse, you can place them in a wicker basket and hold that over the smoke, watching the smoke moving through the basket-weave and surrounding your crystals. The process feels like a ritual for your crystals, and you may want to gently circle the basket anticlockwise in the smoke, which is the direction of releasing. Once you have cleansed your crystals you can use the incense to purify the room.

Let the charcoal burn itself out on the censer in a safe place, such as a stainless-steel sink or in a firepit outdoors. Be aware that a charcoal disc can still be red-hot on the inside, even when the outer surface looks cold and grey. Wait until it has finished burning and has turned to cold ash throughout, before throwing the remains in the dustbin.

Joss sticks are an alternative to solid incense, although many of them are scented with artificial fragrances that will not have a cleansing effect. Check the one that you use has all-natural ingredients.

Smudge

Bundles of herbs, called smudge sticks, are an alternative to incense. There is a long history of burning herbs for purification in many cultures, and smudging comes from Native American tradition. Smudge sticks are made with a variety of dried herbs bound tightly together in a bundle. Blends usually include traditional cleansing herbs, such as sweetgrass, cedar or juniper, but the most popular herb is sage, so some people call the act of smudging "saging". The variety of sage used is Californian white desert sage, which is different from the sage grown in herb gardens for cooking. Desert sage burns with a cleaner smell and has a strongly protective and purifying action. Be aware that white sage is increasingly rare in the wild, and unethical harvesting for smudge sticks adds to its scarcity. It is possible to buy sage smudge that has been harvested ethically and sustainably.

You will need something to hold the smudge stick over, otherwise smouldering leaves could detach themselves and float down to burn holes in your floor covering. Smudge is sometimes sold with large abalone shells for this purpose. These shells look beautiful, with iridescent shining colours on the inside; however, abalone has been over-fished and it is unfortunately endangered. A fireproof dish works just as well and is preferable for most vegetarians and vegans. If you find it difficult to put your smudge stick out, you can add a little sand to the bottom of the bowl. It is also helpful to have a large feather, or to use a feather fan, to direct the smoke.

When you are ready, hold the stalky end of the smudge stick and light the leafy end over your dish. Let the flame burn for a few moments and then gently blow it out, so that the leaves are just smouldering. Now you can hold your crystals in the rising plume of smoke or hold the smudge under a wicker basket to cleanse lots of crystals at once. You can use the feather to gently waft the smoke across your whole crystal collection and around places where you sit or lie down. Once you have finished, stub out the smudge stick and ensure it goes fully out, so that you don't waste any or cause a fire hazard. If you want to make your smudge stick last a lot longer, you can simply detach a couple of leaves from the stick and let them smoulder in your dish.

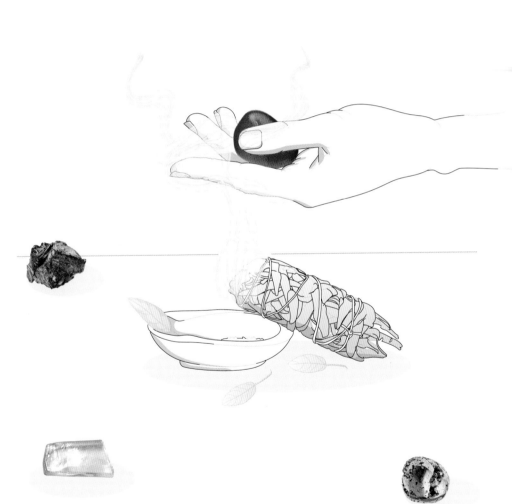

Sound

Sound can send a vibration rippling through your crystals to cleanse them of heavy energies. The most popular sound tools for cleansing crystals are singing bowls, but you could use bells, gongs, drums or rattles instead. If you don't have a percussion instrument you can simply clap your hands crisply around your crystals.

Singing Bowls

Singing bowls vary enormously in size, quality, tone and price. Generally, the larger the singing bowl, the deeper and more resonant the sound will be. To find a singing bowl that "sings" well for you, it is best to shop in person. You shouldn't hit a singing bowl with the mallet to make it sing; instead rub the mallet continuously around the side of the bowl, keeping an even pressure. Sound should start to emerge and build in volume. You can wash and dry a singing bowl if it is dirty, but don't be tempted to polish it; the patina enriches the sound.

Playing the singing bowl around your crystals gives them a cleansing sound-bath. Some people like to place crystals to be cleansed inside the singing bowl before sounding it, which works, although the vibrating crystals can sound unpleasant. It can also be damaging for delicate and softer crystals.

Crystal singing bowls are made from crushed, heated and re-formed quartz and are available in a wide range of sizes and thicknesses, which have been tuned to different notes. Choose your bowl in person so that you know you'll enjoy the sound. Crystal singing bowls are normally used as sound-healing tools, but if you have one, playing it can also be cleansing for your crystals. These bowls can be fragile and need to be handled and played with care. Do not cleanse crystals inside a crystal singing bowl, as the vibrating stones could cause the bowl to shatter.

Essences

Essence sprays are created with the energy signatures of gems, flowers or herbs and can be a convenient way to cleanse your crystals. Several producers make sprays especially for cleansing and purifying. The essence is held in water and is usually preserved in alcohol. Sometimes essential oils or floral waters are added, for fragrance. You don't need to wet your crystals with the spray; simply mist the essence over the crystals. This makes essences a suitable method for all but the most water-sensitive crystals. Keep the spray bottles out of direct sunlight in a cool place, and don't store them near sources of EMFs, such as mobile phones or computers, as these can spoil the energy.

Essences are also available in dropper bottles, which can make them more economical to use. You can add a couple of drops to water in a bowl for washing your crystals, or add drops to water in a spray bottle. Keep the spray in the fridge unless you are adding a preservative, and make a fresh batch once a week, so it doesn't go off.

Salt

Salt has a long and venerable history as a cleansing and purifying substance. It is a stronger cleanser than most crystals will ever need. It can be corrosive and take the surface shine off some crystals. Never use salt to cleanse crystals with H_2O in their formula, as salt can draw out the water content. Opals, for example, could dry and lose their colour-play.

It is best to save salt cleansing as a last resort for a crystal that you can't get to feel clean, even after using other cleansing methods. Use a small bowl of sea salt and cover the crystal in it for a day or two. Throw the salt away afterwards.

The Earth

If a crystal feels like it needs a complete rest, then a final option is to bury it in the ground and let the Earth take care of its energies. If you are burying a crystal and will want to retrieve it, remember to make a note of where you buried it and mark the spot. This is a kind but slow cleansing method that may take weeks or even months. Be aware that this method may damage water-sensitive crystals, and of course your crystal will need physically washing when you retrieve it.

Charging Crystals

Charging is a way of infusing crystals with energy. They don't need charging every time you use them, but they appreciate being charged regularly. Sometimes you'll sense that your crystal needs charging because its energy feels flat and dull, even after cleansing. It may have been working hard for you and needs an energy boost.

Sunlight

The easiest way to charge most crystals is to put them outside in the sunshine. Just as the sunlight cheers our spirits, it energizes crystals and makes them feel more vibrant. If you have a small crystal collection you can put them out in the sunshine often. Larger collections take more time to care for, and you may only be able to charge all your crystals a few times a year; however, the crystals you use most often can be charged more frequently.

If you don't have a garden, you can place your crystals on a sunny windowsill instead. Window glass filters out some of the Sun's rays, but they will still benefit. Be aware that there is a small, but real, risk of fire when putting clear quartz in full sunshine on a windowsill. Sunlight can shine on the crystal in such a way that the rays become tightly focused, as if through a lens. If the light beam shines on combustible material, such as paper, a fire can start. It is the same way that Scouts are taught to light a fire by focusing sunlight using a magnifying glass. Polished clear quartz, especially a sphere, is most likely to focus light like this.

Some crystals are light-sensitive. While a few hours of bright sunshine are unlikely to have much effect, leaving them exposed to the Sun can fade their colours over time. Amethyst and fluorite are particularly susceptible to fading, so don't leave them on a windowsill for long periods.

Moonlight

Crystals can be charged under the light of a full moon on a clear night. The Moon's rays are made of reflected light and so are much softer than the Sun's, but they still contain enough energy to charge your crystals. Some crystals with gentle energies prefer moonlight, including moonstone and selenite. Be aware of selenite's sensitivity to water. Don't put it outside if rain is forecast, and bring it in before dew can form. Moon-bathing crystals on a windowsill doesn't carry any risk of fire.

Charging with Other Crystals

If the sky is cloudy and the Sun and Moon are nowhere to be seen, you can still charge your crystals. Place those ones in need of a boost into a cleansed amethyst geode or onto a bed of amethyst. Leave them to charge for a couple of days, for best effect. Alternatively, place the crystals on a quartz cluster. Bear in mind that amethyst and quartz are quite hard and may scratch softer stones.

You can use clear quartz points to create a charging grid to boost your crystals. You need the quartz points that you are using to be cleansed and charged first. You can use three points arranged as a simple triangle, four points as a square, or as many as you like in a circle. Place them around the crystals that you'd like to charge, with their points directed toward the crystals. The time it takes for your crystals to charge will depend on the number, size and energy of the quartz points.

Dedicating Crystals

Dedicating your crystals is optional, but it helps to set the tone for your work with crystals. A dedication means making a sacred commitment to use the crystals in ways that honour their qualities and are aligned with your highest ethical principles. You should only need to dedicate each crystal once, as a dedication doesn't wash off when you cleanse your crystals. Ideally you will dedicate each new crystal that you add to your collection as a way of welcoming it, but if you have lots of crystals already and want to begin the process, you can dedicate them in groups.

Dedicating a crystal can be as simple as sitting quietly with a cleansed crystal and saying a few special words of blessing or a prayer over it, such as, "I dedicate this crystal in the service of the Light. May it always work for the highest good of all."

Creating an Altar

Altars provide a point of focus for a ceremony. You can make a temporary altar for a dedication ritual, or you could set up a permanent altar that can be activated whenever you wish to spend time in meditation or healing. Over time, a permanent altar can create an atmosphere of sacred space in a room.

First, decide where your altar will be set up, and clean and tidy the room. Choose a piece of furniture to set your altar on. Give it a clean, and make sure you clear out any clutter and tidy the contents, if you are using a cupboard or a set of drawers. Cleanse and purify the energy around the altar with smudge, incense, sound or an essence spray.

Choose a clean cloth to cover your altar, preferably one that hasn't been used for anything else, or one that can be kept aside for this purpose from now on. Your choice of colour helps to sets the tone of your altar. For instance, white symbolizes purity; green reflects nature and growth; yellow radiates happiness; blue is the colour of expansiveness; and violet gives a meditative feel.

Now gather the things you want to place on your altar and arrange them in a way that pleases you. Choose items to represent the four elements: Earth, Air, Fire and Water. The elements were believed to be the fundamental building blocks of creation by the Ancient Greeks, and honouring the elements is still important in many spiritual traditions today.

Air needs to be represented symbolically because it is invisible and around us all the time. A feather is a popular choice, as it represents the birds of the air. A few grains of solid incense, an incense stick or a leaf from a smudge stick can also be used, as the rising smoke makes the air currents visible. Ensure you place your choice in a fireproof holder so that you won't burn your altar cloth.

Fire is usually represented by lighting a candle. The colour is up to you, but white is a good all-round choice for an altar. You can use any size of candle, from a large church candle to a tealight in a holder.

Water can represent itself. Choose a clean dish of a size and design that suit your altar, preferably one you can keep for sacred use. The water can be tap water, but it feels more special to use spring water, whether you collect that yourself or use bottled spring water.

Earth can be represented by a cleansed crystal, as crystals come from the Earth. Alternatively, place a small dish of earth on your altar.

Add an image, sculpture or sacred symbol to represent the divine. It might be the goddess Kuan Yin, the Buddha, an angel, a cross or an ankh (the Ancient Egyptian symbol of life).

You may want to add some flowers, or a sprig of fresh herbs, to represent the natural world and fresh living energy.

Creating a Dedication Ritual

Contemplate the content of your ceremony. You can keep the words and the ceremony short and sweet, simply connecting with the crystal and then placing it on your altar while saying something along the lines of, "I dedicate this crystal to work in love and light, for the highest good of all." Or you can perform a more elaborate dedication ceremony like the one described opposite. You can personalize it to reflect your beliefs, if you want to.

If you like to work with the Moon's cycles you might choose a new moon for your ceremony to welcome a new crystal to your collection. Do make sure you choose a time when you won't be disturbed.

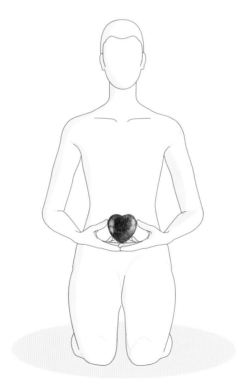

A Sample Dedication Ceremony

1. Get ready by having a shower or a bath and changing into clean clothes. Before you start the ceremony, prepare your energy by grounding, centring and protecting (see pages 36–45). Make sure all the crystals you wish to dedicate have been cleansed (see page 66) and are beside the altar.

2. Activate your altar by lighting the candle and the incense or smudge, if you are using them.

3. Pick up the first crystal you wish to dedicate and hold it quietly for a moment to connect with it, then hold it in the smoke from the incense or smudge, or waft air across it with a feather and say, "I bless this crystal with the element of Air."

4. Now hold the crystal carefully above the flame of the candle and say, "I bless this crystal with the element of Fire."

5. Next hold the crystal over the bowl of water and sprinkle a few drops over it (or simply hold it over the water dish, if it is water-sensitive), saying, "I bless this crystal with the element of Water."

6. Now touch the crystal to your altar crystal or the bowl of earth and say, "I bless this crystal with the element of Earth."

7. Finally, focus on divinity. Hold the crystal in front of you level with your third eye (see page 96) and say, "I dedicate this crystal to the service of the divine [you can name the divinity here, if you work with a specific god / goddess]. May this crystal work only for my highest good and the highest good of all concerned." Place the crystal on your altar and let it soak up the positive vibrations you have created, before it joins the rest of your collection. If it is a permanent altar, it could be nurtured there for a week or more. Leaving your new crystal on the altar reminds you to attune to it (see page 61) and find out more about it.

8. If you have more crystals to dedicate, repeat the ceremony for each one. Stop if you sense you are getting tired and resume the process another day.

5

CRYSTALS AND YOUR ENERGY

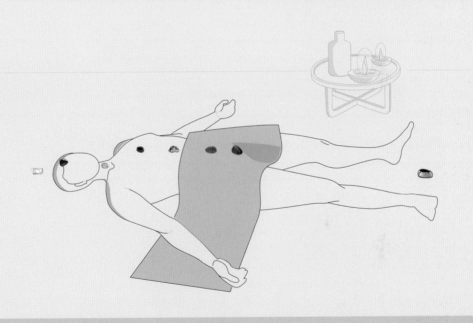

Crystals and Your Chakras

Chakras can be thought of as vortices that bring life-force energy, or *prana*, into the body. The seven largest chakras form a column of energy centres aligned with the spine. These range from the base chakra at the bottom of your spine to the crown chakra at the top of your head. When your chakras are balanced, they will all be spinning and of a similar size as they process energy. If a chakra isn't functioning well, the area of the body that the chakra serves will become depleted or sick. Keeping your chakras clear and well balanced can have a positive effect on your overall wellbeing. Crystals are excellent allies in clearing the chakras and correcting their spin.

The chakras are interconnected. When you focus on healing one chakra, you may have an influence on the way another chakra is functioning. You'll probably have one or two chakras that you will identify as having more issues and needing more attention than the others. Most people have some chakras that are weaker and others that are stronger.

Each chakra has a front and back aspect, apart from the base and crown chakras. This means that blockages might be at the rear of a chakra. Sometimes you may want to place your chosen crystal on the back of a chakra or lie on top of a crystal. Pick a smooth stone if you are lying on it.

Each chakra has an array of attributes, including an associated endocrine gland. Knowing which endocrine gland is connected with each chakra can be helpful when you have a physical health issue. For example, the throat chakra relates to the thyroid, so if you have thyroid issues you may want to try some crystal healing for your throat chakra. While reading about the chakras, consider the major challenges and patterns you have had in your life and which chakras are likely to have been affected.

In the West, the chakras are normally associated with the rainbow of colours, from red at the base to violet at the crown. The rainbow colours are useful when you are learning about the chakras as they can simplify your choice of crystals; however, these colours are not the only ones associated with the chakras. Sometimes crystals of different colours will be more useful for you, and so the crystals mentioned for each chakra are only suggestions.

You will probably find most sensations arise in the first 10–20 minutes after placing the crystals. Once the energy has settled, you can remove the crystals. If you feel there are a lot of issues affecting a chakra, then work on that chakra over time, rather than trying to do all the healing at once.

Occasionally, when you focus on a chakra using crystals, you may stimulate memories of difficult experiences that affected the chakra, or may feel some uncomfortable sensations. If this happens, don't worry – it is usually a sign that some old trauma is ready to be acknowledged, healed and released. Breathe deeply and calmly and allow the crystalline energy to do its work. If the memories being stirred are too upsetting, or the sensations too painful, remove the crystals, have a rest and a drink of water. You can try again later, or you might want to seek the help of a qualified therapist in resolving the issue.

In addition to the seven main chakras there are a great number of minor chakras, so called because they are smaller. Examples include those in the palms of your hands and the soles of your feet, beside your ears, at your naval and the higher heart chakra, located between the heart and throat chakras. You may sense that you need to place crystals on some of your minor chakras. Go with your intuition.

The transpersonal chakras are situated off the body. The Earth star chakra, located under your feet, helps with your grounding. The soul star and stellar gateway chakras are above your head – ensure you are well grounded before you work with them. The stellar gateway is at the top of your aura and receives cosmic energy from the universe. The soul star is situated between the stellar gateway and the crown chakra. It moderates the energies coming through the stellar gateway to a level you can cope with at this stage in your development. Like a transformer on a laptop cable, it protects you and prevents "high-voltage" frequencies from "blowing your fuses".

Understanding more about chakras – and using crystals to keep them working at their optimum – can make a difference to your physical, emotional, mental and spiritual health.

The Base Chakra

Sanskrit name: *Muladhara*, meaning root support
Element: Earth
Endocrine glands: Adrenals
Affirmation: I am safe and secure

The base chakra is also called the root chakra, which is a reminder that it has a role in grounding. It is located at the very base of your spine. A strong base chakra helps you feel safe and secure. It provides an anchor for your energy system as you work with higher vibrational energies.

The base chakra relates to your physical health and the strength of your skeletal system, which is the foundation of your physical body. It is also linked to the adrenal glands. The adrenals produce a range of hormones, including the anti-inflammatory hormone cortisol and the stress hormones adrenaline and noradrenaline, which produce the "fight or flight" response. When stress hormones are released, your body goes into survival mode, preparing you to stand and fight or run away. While this mechanism might be lifesaving in a dangerous situation, the pressures of busy modern lifestyles can stimulate a regular stress response. Other bodily functions, such as your immune system, are affected by prolonged stress. Strengthening your base chakra can help you deal with a stressful situation in a calm and rational way.

Base chakra

Working with Crystals and Your Base Chakra

The same crystals that were recommended for grounding can strengthen your base chakra (see page 38). Choose from red, brown and black crystals and those that contain iron in their chemical formula. Favourites include garnet, which helps you appreciate the abundance of gifts given to you by the Earth; ruby, which promotes endurance; and haematite, which is anchoring and strengthening for your energy.

If lying down, place your chosen crystal at your base chakra between your legs. If sitting, you can sit upon a smooth crystal. Now close your eyes and focus your attention on your base chakra. Imagine breathing energy down into the chakra and visualize a red light glowing there. As you focus on your base chakra you notice the light is expanding and shining more brightly. You may feel warmth or tingling, which is a good sign that your base chakra is responding to the crystal. Know that you are safe and secure in this moment.

Note: If you are using crystals with a friend, put matching crystals at the top of the thighs on a level with the root chakra instead, to avoid embarrassment.

Kundalini energy is normally dormant at the base of the spine. Once awakened, it is a strong rising energy that ultimately needs to flow through the column of the chakras to the crown. This is part of the enlightenment process. If Kundalini is stirring, work through your chakras with crystals to clear any blockages that may cause discomfort and impede its progress. Other disciplines, such as Kundalini yoga, may assist you if you have a Kundalini awakening.

Lifestyle Choices that Support the Base Chakra

- Physical activity, especially outdoors
- Gardening
- Eating a sustaining, healthy diet
- Taking time out for rest and relaxation

The Sacral Chakra

Sanskrit name: *Svadhisthana*, meaning one's own abode
Element: Water
Endocrine glands: Ovaries and testes
Affirmation: I take sensual pleasure in my life

The sacral chakra is located in the lower belly below the naval and is associated with sexuality. The words "sacral" and "sacred" share the same root. This tells us that sex in its highest aspect is a sacred act, and that this part of the body is to be revered. The sacral is also linked to the urinary system.

The sacral is an emotional centre in our body. Like water, your emotions are healthiest when they can flow. Engage fully with your feelings. This will help you to feel more pleasure and joy in life, and to process unhappy experiences too.

This chakra is our centre of creativity. Creating a new life in the womb is perhaps the ultimate act of creation, although all creativity involves the sacral chakra. It flourishes when you provide its energy with a creative outlet.

Enjoyment of the physical body is a gift of the sacral chakra. Find ways to take pleasure in your body that you find relaxing and enjoyable, whether that is dance, swimming, massage or intimacy. Let your mind relax and bring your centre of awareness out of your head and down into your body.

Sacral chakra

Working with Crystals and Your Sacral Chakra

Orange and brown crystals are supportive of the sacral chakra, as are those crystals with a watery nature. Favourite choices include sunstone, which encourages exploration of your creative talents; moonstone, which helps you feel more receptive; and carnelian, which is invigorating and confidence-boosting. If you are working through grief, you may want to choose Apache-tear obsidian or jet. This chakra can hold a lot of stuck emotion, so have tissues to hand and allow your tears to flow if they come.

If you have three pieces of your chosen crystal, you can lie down and place them in a downward-pointing triangle on your lower belly. Otherwise place one crystal on the sacral chakra. If you are seated, simply hold one of the crystals to your sacral chakra. Close your eyes and breathe into your lower belly. Visualize an orange light glowing there. As you breathe you may sense your sacral chakra responding to the crystal by becoming warmer or feeling more relaxed and the light may shine more brightly. Know that you are a sensual and creative being.

Lifestyle Choices that Support the Sacral Chakra

- Belly dance, or other rhythmic dance that gets your hips swaying
- Having sex with a loving partner
- Enjoying a full body massage
- Pursuing creative hobbies

The Solar Plexus Chakra

Sanskrit name: *Manipura*, meaning city of jewels

Element: Fire

Endocrine gland: Pancreas

Affirmation: I am empowered

The solar plexus chakra is situated above the naval and below the sternum. It is a powerhouse of energy and supports your physical vitality. Think of its Fire element as being like the furnace that fuels the rest of the body.

A healthy solar plexus is reflected in self-assurance. It gives a feeling of positivity and optimism and supports a sense of empowerment. This is your centre of will, and it needs to be engaged if you are to accomplish your goals.

Physically the solar plexus relates to the stomach and digestion in general. It is associated with the pancreas, which produces the hormone insulin, which enables us to metabolize glucose. Most of the cells in our bodies use glucose and it is the main fuel for the brain. Using crystals may stabilize your energy levels, although a healthy diet is still required. There isn't a crystal that will "fix" a sugary diet.

Your solar plexus can give you a "gut reaction" about a situation. It is rarely wrong, and listening to your gut can help you avoid costly or painful mistakes. Science is catching up with the idea that there is intelligence located around the area of your solar plexus. The gut is rich in nerve cells and is in two-way communication with the brain via the gut–brain axis. This may explain why stress and worry have an effect on appetite and digestion.

Solar plexus chakra

Working with Crystals and Your Solar Plexus Chakra

Yellow and gold crystals are usually supportive for the solar plexus chakra. Favourites include citrine, which has a happy and positive energy; honey or yellow calcite for the feeling of joy and playfulness they hold; and pyrite, which strengthens the will to take positive action.

Hold or place your chosen crystal on your abdomen above your navel and below your breastbone. If you are attracted to using several crystals, lie down and place the largest in the centre and arrange the others around it. Close your eyes and breathe deeply into your solar plexus. Visualize a glowing golden light there. As you watch, the light expands and glows more brightly until it feels like you have a golden sun shining at your centre. Know that you have the power within you to achieve your goals.

Lifestyle Choices that Support the Solar Plexus Chakra

- Eating a healthy diet with low levels of refined sugars
- Taking note of, and trusting, your gut instincts
- Acting in integrity with your personal beliefs
- Doing martial arts such as Tai Chi, which strengthen your sense of personal power

The Heart Chakra

Sanskrit name: *Anahata*, meaning unstruck or unhurt
Element: Air
Endocrine gland: Thymus
Affirmation: I give love and receive love

The heart chakra is located in the centre of your chest on a level with your physical heart. It is a place of balance between the lower, more physical chakras and the higher, more spiritual chakras. The element of Air reflects the lightness of being and freedom that an open heart brings to life.

Physically the heart chakra influences the heart and lungs, both of which expand and contract rhythmically throughout our lives. The heart is often referred to as the "seat of the soul". Several ancient cultures elevated the heart's importance over the mind. "Listen to your heart" is not a quaint saying; it acknowledges that you have wisdom located there.

The heart chakra is linked to the thymus gland behind the breastbone. This is important for the immune system. It is largest in childhood and starts to atrophy from puberty onward. It is theorized that keeping the thymus as active as possible may slow the ageing process.

The heart chakra is associated with love. If it is closed, due to past hurts, it shuts off the potential for new love to enter your life. We don't become whole-hearted by avoiding emotional pain, but by coming to terms with our feelings so that we can open our hearts to love again.

Heart chakra

Working with Crystals and Your Heart Chakra

Green and pink crystals are often chosen for healing the heart chakra, providing a vast range of possible options. Favourites include rose quartz, which is the archetypal stone of love; aventurine, which carries the hope of new beginnings; and rhodocrosite to promote kindness and heal old wounds.

Lying down, place your chosen heart crystal over your breastbone in the centre of your chest, or simply hold it to your heart centre if you are sitting. Close your eyes and breathe deeply and evenly. Become aware of the air flowing in and out of your lungs and the beating of your heart. Now visualize a glowing green light in the centre of your chest. As you relax into your heart's energy you will see the light expanding and shining more brightly. Know that you are lovable and have love to give.

Lifestyle Choices that Support the Heart Chakra

- Enjoying the unconditional love you share with a pet or a small child
- Sharing a loving hug or embrace
- Treating yourself with love and compassion
- Doing deep-breathing exercises

The Throat Chakra

Sanskrit name: *Vishuddha*, meaning purification
Element: Ether
Endocrine glands: Thyroid and parathyroid
Affirmation: I live my life with truth and integrity

The throat chakra is located in the hollow at the base of the throat. Its primary function is clear communication. Being able to express yourself freely is a sign of a healthy throat chakra. It isn't how much you speak, but the quality and integrity of your communication that count.

Alongside expression, the throat chakra is about being heard and listening attentively to others. A healthy throat chakra also helps you discern whether someone else is speaking truthfully.

The throat chakra relates to the function of the thyroid and parathyroid glands. These produce hormones that control our metabolism. An overactive thyroid will make your metabolism run faster, so that you might feel irritable or anxious, and have unexplained weight loss. An underactive thyroid can make you feel lethargic or depressed, and you may gain weight easily.

If you suffer from sore throats, laryngitis or have a thyroid issue, ask yourself whether you have been keeping your truth hidden. Do you need to express yourself more openly? Have you been keeping quiet to keep the peace? It is also possible that you are being given a signal to speak less and listen more.

Throat chakra

Working with Crystals and Your Throat Chakra

Crystals can be used to soothe the throat and ease clear and honest expression. Typical crystals for healing the throat chakra are blue stones, ranging from pale sky-blue to deeper shades. Favourite choices include calming blue lace agate, refreshing aquamarine and sapphire, which supports truthful communication.

Place your chosen crystal in the hollow of your throat, if you are lying down, or hold it to your throat when sitting up. Become aware of your breathing and notice the air passing through your throat. Visualize a blue light at your throat glowing a peaceful sky-blue. As you watch, the light expands and shines more brightly. Know that you can express yourself with truth and integrity.

Lifestyle Choices that Support the Throat Chakra

- Speaking the truth, even if you must find a tactful way to do so
- Avoiding engaging in gossip and hearsay
- Practising listening with full and undivided attention to what someone is telling you
- Singing or chanting

The Brow Chakra

Sanskrit name: *Ajna*, meaning to know or command
Element: Light
Endocrine gland: Pineal
Affirmation: I perceive clearly

The brow chakra is sometimes referred to as the "third eye" and is located above and between your physical eyes. Its primary role is perception. Physically, the brow chakra relates to your eyes and helps you filter the information that comes in via sight. You see more with your eyes than you could ever process with your mind and notice only those things that seem most relevant. The brow chakra helps you discern what is important.

A healthy brow chakra helps you look upon life's dramas from a more detached viewpoint. You can gain clear insight into what is really happening beneath the surface of a situation.

The brow chakra relates to the pineal gland, which produces the hormone melatonin, helping us to feel relaxed and ready for sleep. Although this pea-sized gland is located deep in the centre of the brain, it is light-sensitive and exposure to daylight helps us to establish our circadian rhythm, or body clock.

A strong brow chakra can produce light, colour, patterns and images. If this becomes distracting, imagine the chakra as the third eye and visualize closing your third eyelid. Clairvoyant symbols and images are only one way you may receive impressions, so don't be despondent if you don't experience visions.

Looking within has always been an important part of the spiritual quest. You may receive insights when you work with the brow chakra.

Brow chakra

Working with Crystals and Your Brow Chakra

Deep-blue stones are classic choices for the third eye, but purple crystals can also be useful. Favourites include lapis lazuli, which helps you connect with your inner wisdom; sodalite for discernment and insight; and lepidolite, which can calm an overactive brow chakra.

Lie down and place your chosen crystal on your brow, or sit and hold the crystal in place. Relax and breathe deeply. Close your eyes and sense the space above and between your eyebrows. Visualize an indigo-blue light glowing here. You may start to see some other coloured light or images. Try not to strain or grasp at any insights that come to you; just relax and notice what you are shown or sense. Imagine the light expanding and shining brighter. Know that you can perceive the truth.

Lifestyle Choices that Support the Brow Chakra

- Forming images in visualizations with as much colourful detail as you can
- Creating something visually appealing, whether that's colouring, arranging flowers or decorating a cake
- Looking at something with your full attention, such as a flower or a crystal
- Keeping a dream diary and noting the symbols that arise

The Crown Chakra

Sanskrit name: *Sahasrara*, meaning thousand-fold
Element: Thought
Endocrine gland: Pituitary
Affirmation: I am awake and aware

The crown chakra is located at the top of your head. It is symbolized as a lotus flower with a thousand petals to represent the opening of higher consciousness. As you awaken, you become aware of a sense of harmony and have the realization that although this world seems full of drama and change, there is an eternal realm of peace that has always been there. This is the true home of your spirit, and to merge into oneness with the divine is your ultimate destiny.

The crown chakra is associated with the pituitary gland, which is sometimes called the "master gland" because it controls the output of the other endocrine glands. Healing energy enters the crown and moves through the column of the chakras to be distributed. Ensure you are well grounded, with a strong base chakra to anchor the energy, before working with the crown chakra.

Through your crown you make your connection to the divine and to your Higher Self. When your crown chakra is functioning well, you may receive inspiration and guidance. You may also become aware of more synchronicity in your life.

Crown chakra

Working with Crystals and Your Crown Chakra

Crystals chosen to clear and develop the crown chakra are often transparent or purple. Favourites include danburite to strengthen your awareness of spiritual guidance; amethyst for purification; and apophyllite for illumination. These are all high-vibrational stones. Ensure that you have a grounding stone close to hand in case you feel light-headed.

Either lie down and place your chosen crystal just above your head or, if seated, you can balance it on top of your head. Close your eyes and relax. Take your attention to your crown and imagine a sphere of violet light glowing there. As it shines, you feel your crown chakra gently responding. Perhaps it feels like petals are unfolding or maybe you are aware of tingling, or a feeling like the top of your head is being gently stroked. As you watch the light in your mind's eye, it expands and glows more brightly. Know that you are awakening.

Lifestyle Choices that Support the Crown Chakra

- Meditating
- Developing awareness in the present moment through mindfulness
- Praying
- Spending time in peaceful contemplation

A Chakra Healing Visualization

This visualization gives each of your chakras a crystalline colour infusion. It is easy to adapt and incorporate your favourite crystals. It is best to do this sitting with your back upright, but you can lie down if you will be more comfortable.

1. Close your eyes and take a few deep breaths. See yourself standing in a sunny meadow. Enjoy the warmth of the Sun on your skin. Breathe in the fresh air. Listen to the birdsong. Enjoy the colourful wildflowers around you. The meadow is a safe and relaxing place for you to visit at any time.

2. On the edge of your hearing you notice the sound of the sea. Walk toward it and notice the rhythmic sound of the waves. You come to the edge of a cliff and there below you is a beautiful sandy beach, with the sea glinting in the sunshine. At your feet you can see steps cut into the cliff. You go down the steps, one by one, making your way to the beach. When you reach the bottom, you step out onto the beach.

3. You walk along the beach, enjoying the gentle breeze coming from the sea and the relaxing sound of the waves on the shore. Perhaps you take your shoes off and enjoy the feeling of warm sand under your feet. Maybe you have a paddle in the gently lapping water at the sea's edge.

4. As you wander along the beach you look at the cliff and notice that at the far end of the beach there is a cave. Walk along the beach to the cave. You go inside and see a large smooth black stone in the centre, which looks like an inviting place to sit. Although it is quite dark the cave feels very safe and you can see the cave mouth with the bright beach beyond. You become aware that there are hundreds of crystals glittering in the cave walls.

5. As you relax, some of the crystals begin to glow with a ruby-red light. Their light is filling the cave. You breathe in the ruby-red energy and sense your base chakra soaking up the light. You feel the ruby energy warming and revitalizing you. You feel strengthened by the light. When you have absorbed as much of the ruby light as you need, the crystals begin to dim and the light fades.

6. You are in the dark cave once more, and now other crystals begin to light up. They emit a sparkling orange light, the light of sunstone. The cave is infused with orange light and you breathe in the colour. You sense your sacral chakra soaking up the light, feeling it warming and quickening. You are aware of your sensual nature. You know that you have talents and abilities that are ready for creative expression. When you have absorbed as much of the sunstone energy as you desire, the crystals begin to dim, the light fades and the cave is dark again.

7. Now yellow light begins to shine from citrine crystals in the cave walls. The citrine light fills the cave like golden sunshine. You breathe in the golden light and sense your solar plexus chakra soaking up the citrine energy. You feel warmed, energized and empowered and know you can achieve your goals. When you

have absorbed as much citrine light as you need, the crystals begin to dim and the light fades.

8. You are in the darkened cave once more and now you notice emerald crystals lighting up around you and emitting their vibrant green light. The cave is flooded with vivid green light and you breathe it in. You sense your heart chakra soaking up the emerald energy. You feel your heart opening wider to drink in the light. You sense love and compassion filling your heart. When you have absorbed as much emerald light as you need, you see the crystals begin to dim and the light fades.

9. Now the darkness of the cave is softly lit by aquamarine crystals, which emit a watery blue light. The cave is filled with rippling blue light and you breathe it in. You sense your throat chakra drinking in the aquamarine energy and a sense of refreshment flows through you. You feel the light washing over you, cleansing you and helping you express your thoughts and feelings. When you have bathed in as much aquamarine light as you need, the crystals begin to dim and the light fades.

10. The dark cave is now lit by lapis lazuli crystals, which emit a dark indigo-blue light with golden sparkles that twinkle like stars in the night sky. You breathe in the deep blue-and-gold light and feel your brow chakra opening to absorb the lapis energy. There is a sense of profound wisdom surrounding you. You sense your third eye is being cleared so that you can perceive more deeply. Once you have absorbed as much lapis lazuli energy as you need, the crystals begin to dim and the light fades.

11. The cave is now lit by amethyst crystals, which shine with a violet light. You breathe in the light and sense your crown chakra opening to the amethyst energy. You sense the amethyst light purifying you, helping you release those things that have been holding you back. When you feel you have released enough for the moment, the amethyst crystals begin to dim and the light fades.

12. You are in the darkened cave once more. You realize the smooth stone you have been sitting on is black obsidian and you know it has been grounding you. Sit and relax on the obsidian for as long as you like while you let your energy settle. When you are ready, get up and thank the crystals for the healing you have received. Know that the cave will be there for you whenever you want to return.

13. You step back outside onto the sunny beach and enjoy the fresh air, the sound of the sea and the brightly sparkling light on the waves. Take your time walking back along the beach, enjoying the beautiful surroundings.

14. You come to the steps that lead up the cliff and climb them one by one, all the way up, until you step back into the sunny meadow. Know that the meadow is always there when you want to take time out and relax.

15. Now let the images fade. Take a few deep breaths and open your eyes. Note your experiences in your journal. It is interesting to reflect on which crystalline light you needed the most. You might like to carry that crystal with you or use it for a chakra placement.

Balancing the Chakras

Although you can do a lot of healing by focusing on your weakest chakras, it is helpful to balance the chakras as a complete set. You can do a very simple chakra balance for yourself by using a crystal for each of the rainbow colours, plus a grounding stone, and laying them on the corresponding chakras, with a grounding stone at your Earth star below your feet. However, you will get better results by choosing crystals with an intention to balance your chakras (see below). Use whichever method you feel works best for you.

How to Choose Crystals with the Intention to Balance Your Chakras

1. Start by focusing on your base chakra and set your intention: "Show me a crystal to balance my base chakra." When you have chosen that crystal, put it to one side and move onto your sacral: "Show me a crystal to balance my sacral chakra." Put that crystal above the base crystal, so that you form a line of stones in the order of your chakras. This makes it easier when you are ready to lay them on.

2. Continue to work upward through each of your chakras until you get to your crown. You may feel that one or two of your chakras don't need a crystal placed on them or that you need to place a couple of crystals for some of your chakras. Go with your intuition.

3. It is likely that some of the crystals you select will not match the rainbow colour for the chakra – that is fine. It may be that the chakra needs a crystal of a different colour to achieve balance, or perhaps it needs the crystal you have chosen for its chemical composition or its shape. Don't overthink your choices; crystal healing is not like following a recipe, it is an intuitive art. Accept that there will be a reason why you chose that crystal, even when it isn't obvious.

How to Balance Your Chakras

1. Place your selected crystals in chakra order within easy reach beside you, along with a grounding stone.

2. First, place your grounding crystal at the Earth star below your feet, then lie down and put the crystals on your chakras.

3. Relax and notice how they feel. If any crystal feels uncomfortable, decide whether you are happy to let the process unfold. Remember: crystals can feel heavy or produce strange sensations when they are hard at work. These sensations usually ease off when the crystal has done its job, but if you are finding it too unpleasant, remove the crystal and put it to the side of you. You might want to try it again in a few minutes, but if not, don't worry; it may have been too strong for you at the moment. You can try a different crystal for that chakra next time.

4. If you wish, you can use the energy from your hands to give your chakras some extra healing. Start by placing a hand over your base chakra and intending to give the chakra the energy it needs. After a few minutes or when you feel ready, move your hand to your sacral chakra. Move on through the chakras in this way. You may sense that some chakras want more attention and you need to spend longer with them, while others may require little or no healing. If you aren't sure, give them a few minutes each.

5. It can be interesting to place your hands on two chakras that you feel need to communicate with each other. For example, if your head and your heart feel at odds, place one hand on your brow chakra and another on your heart chakra. If you need to speak what is in your heart, place one hand on your throat chakra and one on your heart chakra.

6. Relax in your chakra layout and notice the sensations change as the crystals work. Usually everything will settle down after 15–20 minutes. You can relax there for ten minutes longer, if you are enjoying it.

7. Once you have finished, take all the crystals off and sit up. Hold your grounding stone if you feel light-headed and have a drink of water. Write up the crystals you used, and your experiences, in your journal.

Crystals and Your Aura

The human aura, or energy field, surrounds the physical body. A healthy aura has a smooth egg shape and is approximately the diameter of the body with the arms outstretched. Its outer boundary forms a naturally protective space for the individual. You intuitively sense when someone has crossed your auric boundary uninvited, and is in your personal space. Although they may not be touching you physically, it feels like they are standing too close and it is unpleasant. The natural reaction is to take a step back from them and restore your boundary.

The outer layer of the aura can become damaged with holes or tears. Sometimes the damage is caused by outbursts of strong emotion; sometimes it comes from other people's anger. Surgical procedures may also damage the aura. Aura damage will usually repair itself over time, but until it has healed it is a breach in your natural protection and your energy can leak, leaving you depleted. Maintaining a daily protection routine will prevent most aura damage.

Your lifestyle choices will affect your aura. Following the usual guidance for a healthy lifestyle will help to keep your energy field strong and vibrant. Your moods and health also affect your aura, so if you have been angry, unhappy, anxious or sick, your aura will mirror that. Empaths and healers need to take special care of their aura, as they have an increased tendency to absorb energies from other people and the environment. If you maintain a daily protection routine, then external energies are unlikely to penetrate your auric boundary, but at times it may still feel like your aura needs a good cleanse. This can help shift lingering bad moods and speed recovery from illness. The more sensitive you are, the quicker you will notice if your energy feels weighed down and in need of attention.

Cleansing Your Aura

Many of the methods described for cleansing crystals are equally useful for aura cleansing (see page 66). Taking a shower, or having a bath, is one of the first steps to try if your energy feels a bit heavy. Dissolving a few handfuls of sea salt in bathwater has an additional purifying effect. You can add some amethyst, aquamarine or clear quartz crystals to your bath to cleanse yourself in crystal waters.

Sound can be a good way to shift stagnant energy from your aura. Play a singing bowl, a drum or shake a rattle around yourself. Combine sound and movement by playing lively music and dancing to shake up and disperse stagnant energy from your aura.

Taking yourself outside into the elements can be cleansing. A walk by a river, a visit to a waterfall or a trip to the seaside can be refreshing. Sunshine can clear smoggy energy from the aura, and a bracing walk on a breezy day is helpful for "blowing away the cobwebs".

How to Cleanse and Repair Your Aura with Selenite

1. Take as many cleansing rounds of breath as you need for each stage of this exercise.

2. Hold a piece of selenite vertically in front of your face. As you breathe in deeply through your nose, imagine you are breathing in selenite's refreshing energy. Visualize the selenite energy cleansing and clearing your lungs. Move your hands away from your face as you breathe out through your mouth, releasing any old stagnant energies with the out-breath.

3. Raise the selenite again for your next in-breath. Visualize the selenite's energy cleansing through your physical body. Move the selenite away as you breathe out old, stale energy.

4. Raise the selenite in front of your face for your next in-breath. Visualize the selenite energy cleansing your aura. Move the selenite away again for the out-breath.

5. To finish, sweep the selenite around the boundary of your aura, which is approximately an arm's length all the way round you. Imagine the selenite is smoothing over any areas you can't reach, including your back and under your feet. Pay particular attention to any places you sense may be damaged. Visualize the selenite repairing any holes or tears and sealing you in a protective white crystalline bubble.

How to Purify Your Aura with Amethyst and the Violet Flame

The violet flame is a cleansing fire that is believed to be a gift to humanity from the Ascended Master St Germain. This cool flame will not burn you, but it will transmute heavy energy. You may find this exercise particularly helpful at the end of a difficult day, after an illness or following an argument.

1. Sit or stand with your back upright, holding a piece of amethyst just in front of your solar plexus chakra. If your crystal has points, these should be held facing upward.

2. Close your eyes and take a few deep breaths. Say aloud, "I call upon St Germain to help me burn the violet flame."

3. In your mind, the amethyst crystal takes on the appearance of a violet flame. At first it is the same size as your crystal, but as you watch, the flame grows and multiplies until tongues of violet fire are filling your entire aura.

4. Intend that you will release as much stagnant, unhealthy energy to the cleansing fire as you can at this time. Imagine yourself feeding the flame with any negative thoughts and emotions you have been holding on to.

5. When you feel you have released enough for the time being, you watch the violet flames die down and withdraw into your amethyst.

6. Visualize shielding the outside of your aura with a shell of amethyst crystal to protect your freshly cleansed energy.

7. Remember to say "Thank you" to St Germain for his gift.

The Subtle Bodies

The aura isn't just one amorphous mass; it has layers that relate to the seven main chakras. These are called the "subtle bodies". Working on the chakras has a corresponding effect on the aura. Like the chakras, the layers can be divided into those that are more physical and those that are more spiritual in nature. The layers closest to the physical body are more tangible as they have a lower vibration. These are the layers that clairvoyants usually see. The more spiritual layers have a higher vibrational energy and so are harder to perceive. The final four layers of the subtle bodies – the astral, causal, soul and spiritual bodies – are rarely perceived even by psychics, as they have such a high vibration, but they all benefit from regular aura cleansing. They may also be supported by working on the corresponding chakra.

The Etheric Body

The first layer of the aura is closest to the physical body and is called the etheric body. It relates to the base chakra and reflects your physical vitality. Someone with good energy levels will have a "bouncy" and bright etheric layer. Most people can be taught to see etheric energy, even if they don't think they are psychic. If you gaze softly at someone sitting or standing against a plain background, you will probably start to perceive an outline of light around them, especially around their head and shoulders.

You can also learn to see the etheric energy that flows from the tips of your fingers and toes. Hold your hands out in front of you against a plain background, palms facing you, with your fingertips parted. With a soft gaze, you may start to perceive a fuzzy or bright outline of energy around your fingers. You may also notice the energy extending from your fingertips. When you hold your hands close together, it will connect your hands at the fingertips. Play with this energy connection, seeing how far you can stretch your hands apart before it is lost.

Boosting your etheric energy with crystals can have a positive effect on your physical vitality. If you feel depleted, you can place crystals on your body while you lie down and relax, or you can wear crystal jewellery, or carry crystals, to support your etheric energy. Grounding with the element of Earth strengthens the etheric body. Choose grounding and energizing crystals such as iron pyrite or red jasper.

The Emotional Body

The emotional body is the next layer of the aura and contains colours that clairvoyants are sometimes shown. If you have been told you have a "green aura", this is the layer they are probably looking at. The emotional body responds to your feelings, and the colours can change according to your mood. This layer relates to the sacral chakra. Its predominant colour will reflect the kind of person you are. Very physical and energetic people are likely to have red and orange auras. Teachers and writers may have a lot of yellow. Those who are healers will often show green or blue. Meditators may have a lot of white or purple. Your aura colours can evolve and change over time, especially if you are on a path of spiritual development.

You don't need to know what colour your aura is, but be aware that heavy emotions can cloud or darken this layer. By using aura-cleansing techniques you can release difficult feelings and move on from upsets more easily. Helpful crystals for the emotional body include rose quartz, moonstone and others that help you get in touch with your feelings. Taking a bath with these crystals can help, as Water is the element that corresponds with the sacral chakra and is good for cleansing emotional energies.

The Mental Body

This layer corresponds to the solar plexus chakra and reflects your thought processes. Keeping the mental body cleansed can help you to think more clearly. Those who perceive the mental body describe it as a bright yellow, when healthy. If you get bogged down in negative thinking, this layer can become congested and it becomes harder to shift out of unhelpful thought patterns.

One way of clearing the mental body is to use a simple fire ceremony, because Fire is the element that relates to the solar plexus chakra. First, write all your repeating negative thoughts down on paper. Write in "stream of consciousness" – don't stop to reread, correct your spelling or punctuation, just let the words flow out of you. Now take your papers, along with matches or a lighter, outdoors to a fireproof container such as a firepit. Put the sheets of paper into the container one at a time, lighting them carefully and watching them burn. You should feel lighter and less burdened as a result. If you need to, you can repeat this exercise once or twice a week until the negative thought patterns have cleared.

Using golden or yellow crystals can clarify and uplift your thought processes. Good choices include citrine and rutilated quartz. Having these crystals with you when you need to deliver a presentation or sit an exam can help you focus and think positively.

The Astral Body

The astral body relates to the heart chakra and reflects the state of close personal relationships. As the heart chakra corresponds to the element of Air, going out in the fresh air to cleanse the aura can be an effective method to use. Crystals offering emotional healing, such as rhodocrosite and morganite, provide helpful support for the astral body.

The Causal Body

The causal body relates to the throat chakra. It is believed that the causal body holds information about our life purpose and keeps us on track as our plans unfold. Clairvoyants have described this layer as cobalt-blue. If you feel confused and don't know how to move forward, your causal body may need cleansing. Sound is a good way of keeping this layer cleansed. Sing, play a singing bowl, drum or chant – whatever feels right for you. Crystals that help with clarity may be supportive for your causal body. Possible choices include clear quartz and sodalite.

The Soul Body

The soul body relates to the third-eye chakra, and those who have seen it report it comprising brilliantly coloured rays of light. At this level we have the ability to perceive ourselves as connected with all that is. If you feel disconnected and separate from the rest of creation, then working on this fine layer of the aura may help. Visualizing a waterfall of multicoloured crystalline light that you can step into can cleanse this layer. Crystals that enhance perception and inner knowledge, such as lapis lazuli or labradorite, may support the soul body.

The Spiritual Body

The final layer of the aura is the spiritual body and this layer forms the naturally protective boundary for the aura. It relates to the crown chakra and is a level at which we know we are One with the divine. Visualizing yourself surrounded by a shimmering golden egg of light can strengthen this layer. If you perceive holes or tears in the aura, either use selenite to smooth over and reinforce your auric boundary or imagine sewing up the tear, using fine but strong golden threads to make your repair. High-vibrational crystals such as selenite or danburite are most useful for the spiritual body.

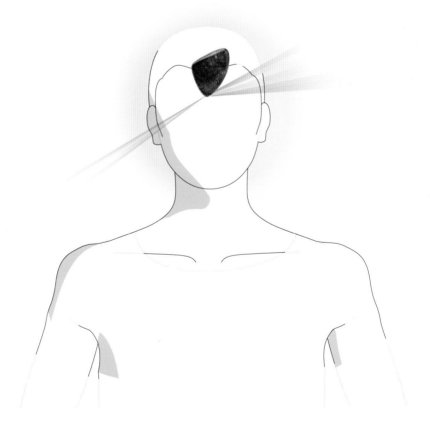

A Gift from Mother Earth Visualization

Work with this visualization to receive crystal healing and guidance. If you have a specific issue that you would like help with, then set your intention at the outset.

1. Make yourself comfortable, take a few deep breaths and close your eyes. Visualize standing on a sunlit woodland path. You hear birdsong and breathe in the fresh air. You follow the path as it meanders through the trees, enjoying the peaceful surroundings.

2. The path leads to a huge tree in a clearing. It is so tall you cannot see the top. At the base of the trunk there is a door that opens for you. Stepping inside, you find yourself in a round room. You see the tree protects an entrance into the Earth, which is lit by a welcoming golden glow. Looking down, you see rough-hewn steps of stone descending in a gentle spiral. You walk down the steps, deeper and deeper into the Earth.

3. At the bottom of the spiral you find yourself in a corridor cut into stone, lit by the same golden light. You walk along the corridor, which leads to a round room, a sanctuary cut into the stone. The golden light is emanating from lit candles set around the room. Although you are deep within the Earth, the air feels fresh and clean and is lightly fragranced with incense.

4. An oak chair awaits you in the centre of the room. It is throne-like and intricately carved, set with precious gems. Sit in the chair now, with your palms held open on your lap. Close your eyes and meditate in this sacred space. As you do so, you sense a weight dropping into your palms and feel the shape of a crystal that has materialized for you.

5. You open your eyes and examine your gift from Mother Earth. Notice the colour, shape and size of your crystal; its texture, any patterning and the way it reflects or absorbs the light of the candles. Do you recognize the crystal? Don't worry if you don't; simply trust that this is the perfect crystal for you today.

6. Sit quietly with your crystal. Intuitively you will know why this crystal has been given to you and you will understand the message it has for you. As you sit with it, you sense the crystal is giving you healing.

7. When you feel the healing is complete, you stand up, still holding your crystal. You humbly thank Mother Earth for her gift and make your way out of the sanctuary back into the corridor. Follow the passageway to the spiral steps and start to make your way back up. Climb all the way until you come out into the room at the base of the tree.

8. Thank the tree for guarding the sacred space and make for the door, which opens again for you. Outside in the daylight you examine the crystal again and then place it carefully in a pouch or a bag so that you can carry it with you. Walk back along the meandering woodland path to your starting place.

9. Take a few deep breaths, have a stretch and, when you are ready, open your eyes. Write up your experience in your journal. If you recognize the crystal you were given you may want to look it up in the Crystal Directory (see pages 172–293).

6

CRYSTALS IN DAILY LIFE

Crystals for Daily Living

You will gain the most benefits from your crystal collection if you use it regularly as part of your daily life. This can be simple, easy and fun to do. Remember the key to choosing crystals is setting a clear intention. Once you know why you want to work with a crystal, the selection process is easy. Let's look at some of the ways you might incorporate your crystals into your life.

Choosing a Crystal for the Day

This is one of the simplest practices, but it can be of immeasurable benefit Whatever your plans, choosing a crystal can help you get the best from your day. Look up a suitable stone in the Crystal Directory (see pages 172–293) or use an intuitive method to make your selection (see pages 52–60). If mornings are too busy, you could choose one the evening before, so that the crystal is ready and waiting for you. It is very quick and easy to choose your crystal of the day by synchronicity. Drawing your crystal of the day out of a lucky-dip bag of crystals is fun and only takes a moment. The whole family can enjoy using this method.

Crystal Jewellery

If you have crystal jewellery you can choose the most appropriate piece for your needs. Keep your crystal jewellery cleansed, so that it is ready to wear. Some crystal jewellery is designed around sacred symbols of harmony and protection. These symbols can invoke the power of beliefs that stretch back thousands of years. If the beliefs resonate with your own, then the symbol can work well for you. If not, then you are unlikely to feel much benefit from wearing it, as you'll be out of integrity with yourself. For example, if you find the symbol of the Cross supportive of your Christian faith, then wearing a crucifix is likely to be strengthening for you; whereas if you are Pagan, you might prefer an ankh or a pentagram.

Wearing gemstone earrings can harmonize the left and right hemispheres of the brain and may influence the third eye too. Earrings can also balance the minor chakras that lie beside your physical ears, that help you to hear subtle messages of guidance.

Crystal necklaces and pendants can support your throat chakra or your heart chakra, depending on the length of the chain. If you are in the habit of centring at your heart, then a pendant worn here can help you stay centred. You can also imagine the energy of the crystal emanating out to fill your whole aura. If you can't find a necklace in your chosen crystal, you can buy a metal spiral cage that can hold a tumblestone and can be worn on a thong or chain.

Crystal bracelets can have an influence on your whole physical system, as the blood flows close to the surface in your wrists and will carry the crystalline energy throughout your body. Beaded power bracelets are available in a wide range of crystals, and are an affordable way to give yourself a selection of crystals to wear for the day. You can even design your own by buying the crystal beads of your choice and stringing them on elastic.

Gemstone rings can support your energy. The belief that a vein from the fourth finger of the left hand ran directly to the heart stretches all the way back to Ancient Egypt. The *vena amoris*, Latin for "vein of love", is the reason why wedding and engagement rings are traditionally worn on this finger in many parts of the world. This isn't the custom everywhere, however, and the fourth finger of the right hand is traditional in other countries. Either way, the fourth finger has become known as the "ring finger". The ring itself can be seen as a symbol of eternity, as it has no beginning and no end, which is why it has been a tradition since ancient times to use a ring to symbolize marriage, rather than a nice pendant or a brooch, for example.

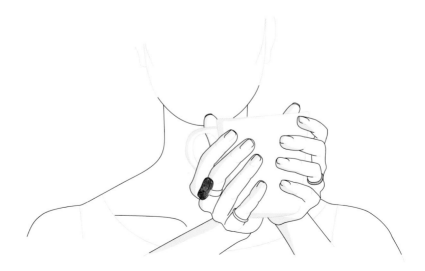

Hindus use the associations of the different fingers in their faith. If you look at portrayals of Hindu gods and goddesses, you will see they are usually shown with specific hand positions called *mudras*. *Mudras* are still used in sacred dance and in yoga today. The associations for each finger may help you decide which finger to wear your gemstone ring on:

- The thumb relates to the planet Mars. Wearing a ring here may support assertiveness and the will to get things done.
- The index finger relates to the planet Jupiter. The energy is of expansiveness and relates to thought. A ring worn on the index finger may help you think more clearly and see possibilities.
- The middle finger relates to the planet Saturn. This energy holds us accountable to a higher power. Wearing a ring here may support your desire to act with integrity.
- The fourth finger is associated with the Sun. Wearing a ring here can support stamina and energy levels in general.
- The little finger is associated with Mercury. A ring on your little finger may ease expression and communication.

According to Traditional Chinese Medicine some of the meridians, or energy channels, flow along the fingers and have their start or end points on the fingertips of each hand:

- The Lung meridian ends on the thumb. Wearing a ring here may help you set healthy boundaries, as well as having a connection to the health of the lungs.
- The Large Intestine meridian starts on the index finger. Wearing a ring on this finger may help you decide what is good to keep in your life and what needs to be let go of, as well as supporting the intestine.
- The Pericardium or Heart Protector meridian ends on the middle finger. Wearing a ring here may help to calm anxiety and support enjoyment of life.
- The Triple Heater meridian starts on the ring finger. This meridian controls the regulation of body heat, so if you are always too hot or too cold, try wearing a ring here.
- The Heart meridian ends on the little finger. Wearing a ring here can support empathy as well as heart health.
- The Small Intestine meridian starts on the little finger. Supporting the energy of this meridian can help you with discernment, as well as assisting with the proper assimilation of food and nutrition.

Creating a Crystal Medicine Bag

Creating a medicine bag is part of Native American tradition. It can contain a range of items that represent "good medicine" for you. The word "medicine" has a much broader meaning than we are used to and doesn't only relate to health, but also to support for wellbeing in general. The bag may include items that represent your guiding spirits. It might contain a crystal, herbs, a small carving of a totem animal, a feather and a pinch of cornmeal, or tobacco. It is normally worn tucked out of sight under clothing.

You can make a personalized crystal medicine bag, which may be worn or carried on your person. The crystals you choose can be small – it is the choice of crystal energies and their combined effect on you that are important. The contents of your medicine bag may be changed over time.

1. First, sew yourself a pouch or buy a ready-made medicine bag. These are usually made from leather and suspended on a thong around the neck, but you can use any material that will keep the contents safe. The pouch should be of a size that will be comfortable to carry on your person. Once you have your bag, you may like to pass it through smudge or incense to cleanse it, ready for use.

2. Set the intention that you are choosing a team of crystals that will be "good medicine" for you. Gather the smaller crystals in your collection to select from. You can use any of the choosing methods to select crystals for your medicine bag, but if you have a helper, then kinesiology (see page 59) is a good way to find the perfect combination. The right crystals tested together should make your muscle-test strong – stronger than for any of the crystals tested individually.

3. Place the crystals in your medicine bag and wear or carry the pouch on your person. Don't forget that the crystals will benefit from regular cleansing and charging. If you want to, you can add other small items that you feel support your energy. Muscle-test them in combination with the crystals to check the overall effect is strengthening.

Crystals in the Workplace

Crystals can support you, whatever you do for a living. If you have a desk in an office where the crystals will be secure, then you can choose a crystal that will inspire you and help you to focus. Crystals are beautiful, so putting one on display will probably attract admiring glances. A smooth boulder of fluorite that you can rest a hand on as you gather your thoughts can help you stay focused and keep you feeling organized. A clear quartz point may help you think and communicate with greater clarity. A piece of obsidian placed at the front of your desk can be visualized as a shield that keeps office politics out of your personal workspace. If you can't display personal belongings at work, use pocket-sized crystals that can travel to and from work with you.

If you have a more physical job and are on your feet all day, then wearing a strengthening crystal such as ruby to help with stamina can be useful. Jewellery is not permitted in some jobs and certain uniforms don't have pockets, so you may need to get creative. A lot of women place a crystal in their bra. Choose a smooth stone and make sure it doesn't give you a strange profile! Some people even stitch little pockets into their underwear to hold their crystals. Ensure you remove any crystals before you throw your clothes in the wash.

Working with others can be trying at times, even when you love your job. If you work with people who are poorly, or have to deal with customer complaints, or have difficult members of staff to interact with, then doing your protection before leaving for work and wearing a protective crystal can help shield your energy. Once you get home at the end of your working day you can detach from any difficult incidents using kyanite. Sweep the kyanite blade down around your aura and imagine any connections to those interactions being cut.

Everyone's job has some challenges, however perfect it may look from the outside, but if work becomes a constant battle or fills you with dread, then it isn't right for you. You spend far too much of your life at work to waste your time in a job that is making you miserable or unwell. Honour yourself by finding a job that suits you better. Your crystals can support you and shield your energy while you look for a more fulfilling job that suits your talents and abilities.

Commuting with Crystals

For many people, the journey to and from the workplace is one of the most stressful parts of the day. Travelling on packed trains or buses brings you up close and personal with complete strangers. If you need to commute, do your protection before you leave the house. Take a deep breath in as you step into a crowd and imagine that you are drawing your aura closer around you. Breathe normally again and then, when you have space around you, blow your breath out and imagine expanding your aura back to its normal size. Wearing or carrying a protective stone such as obsidian or black tourmaline, combined with a calming crystal such as kunzite, may help you feel safer and more peaceful even in rush-hour crowds.

Driving in busy traffic can be stressful. You could choose and dedicate a crystal for use in your car. It might be black tourmaline for protection, clear quartz to help you stay alert, sodalite for discernment on your route or larimar to help you stay calm. Most cars have a cubbyhole or space for small change where you can place a crystal. Make sure it won't roll around or become a dangerous projectile if you need to do an emergency stop. Remember to cleanse your car crystal regularly so that its energy stays fresh.

Crystals for Students

Having an interest in learning helps to keep your mind active and alert throughout your life. Absorbing and memorizing information can be boosted with crystals. Fluorite helps you to focus on the topic and organize facts so that they are stored in a way you can access them. Clear quartz may help you recall information clearly, particularly if you revise while holding the crystal. Taking the crystal you have used during your revision into your exam can jog your memory when you look at it. If you aren't allowed to place items on the exam desk, keep the crystal in your pocket.

For a lot of students going away to university is the first time they have lived independently from their parents. It is both an exciting and a nerve-racking time and a true rite of passage. As a parent, sending your budding student off with a personalized "crystal support kit" feels good. Such a kit might contain:

- Aventurine for new beginnings
- Bloodstone for courage
- Tiger's eye for stability
- Rutilated quartz to sharpen thinking and inspire insightful assignments
- Fluorite to support focus and organization
- Carnelian to boost confidence
- Rose quartz as a reminder that your love goes with them
- Amethyst against intoxication (or at least to help with the hangover!)

Crystals for Stress Relief

Stress can be a killer. It doesn't appear in the lists like heart disease, which is the number-one killer for men, but high stress levels can raise blood pressure and pulse rates, so they may lie behind many heart attacks as well as contributing to a variety of other illnesses.

The world gets ever faster and more pressurized. It is more important than ever to switch off and chill out. Using crystals for stress relief can provide an antidote, giving your body a chance to rest, relax and repair. Ideally, build stress relief into your daily routine. If you don't think you have enough time to relax, it is a good sign that you need to! You can use a favourite crystal visualization, take a crystal bath or try a crystal-healing layout. Setting an intention for stress relief and relaxation will help you choose the perfect crystal for you.

The Seal of Solomon

Lying in a Seal of Solomon layout is an easy way to let go of stress and relax. The Seal of Solomon is also called the Star of David and is an ancient symbol of protection. As well as its sacred use within the Jewish faith, it appears within the symbol for the heart chakra. Formed of two intersecting triangles, it is a well-balanced shape that helps to restore a sense of harmony and equilibrium. The upward-pointing triangle points to the heavens and is masculine in nature, whereas the downward-pointing triangle is feminine and points to the Earth.

You can create the Seal of Solomon using six pieces of any crystal of your choice. When placed around your body, the upward-pointing triangle will have its apex above your head and the other two crystals can be placed on either side of your hips. The downward-pointing triangle will have its point beneath your feet and the other two crystals can be placed on either side of your shoulders. Because of the shape of the human body, your triangles will be elongated, but this won't detract from the healing.

Crystals with natural terminations, such as smoky quartz points or amethyst points, can be directed to point outward from the body first, to relieve stress and release congested energies, then turned round to point inward, once you are feeling more relaxed and ready to replenish and restore your energy. For ease, you can put the crystals into position before you lie down in the shape.

Lie in the Seal of Solomon for as long as you like: 20–30 minutes is usually ample and even a ten-minute layout can be helpful.

To de-stress you might choose:

- Smoky quartz to release tension and help you get grounded
- Amethyst for purification
- Howlite for a sense of peace and restfulness

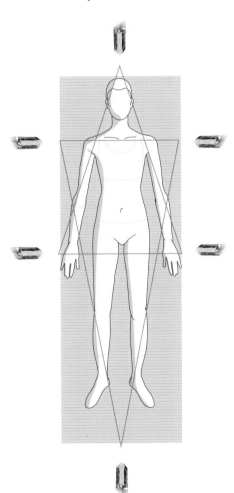

Crystals Around Your Home

Crystals are beautiful and decorative additions to your home. On top of this, they can enhance the energy of the space and make the atmosphere more harmonious for everyone who lives there. As you place your crystals, think about the function of the room, who uses it and the mood you wish to create in that space.

Understanding some of the basic principles of Feng Shui, the ancient Chinese art of placement, can help you make the most of your home and will guide you to the areas that will be best enhanced by crystals. The Chinese refer to subtle energy as chi. According to Feng Shui, chi enters and circulates around the home under the influence of the directions. Each direction is assigned one of the Chinese five elements: Wood, Fire, Earth, Metal and Water. These are the same elements that are used in Chinese Medicine, including acupuncture. Each direction has a potential benefit for a different area of your life. Crystals can help you enhance the area you wish to focus on.

To make Feng Shui enhancements you first need to know which direction your home faces, so use a compass to orient your property and draw up a room plan. The Lo Shu Key (see opposite) expands and contracts to fit over the floor plan of your house, so if, for example, you have a house that is long and narrow, the grid will become a rectangle. If you live in an apartment within a larger building, just use the Lo Shu Key over your space.

Chi needs to circulate smoothly around your home. Think about how you move through your home. Is it easy to navigate? If you need to squeeze past piles of things in corridors or reach across mounds of clutter, then the flow of chi will also be restricted in these places. When you look at the Lo Shu Key you can identify which life area your clutter is having most effect on. That can be a great incentive for a good clear-out and a tidy.

The Lo Shu Key

Prosperity, Blessings and Abundance **SOUTH-EAST** Main cure: Wood Supported by: Water Destroyed by: Metal	Fame and Self-expression **SOUTH** Main cure: Fire Supported by: Wood Destroyed by: Water	Relationships and Marriage **SOUTH-WEST** Main cure: Earth Supported by: Fire Destroyed by: Wood
Family, Elders and Ancestors **EAST** Main cure: Wood Supported by: Water Destroyed by: Metal	Unity and Health **CENTRE** Keep the centre clear; ensure energy circulates easily and is not blocked or drained here	Children and Creativity **WEST** Main cure: Metal Supported by: Earth Destroyed by: Fire
Education and Knowledge **NORTH-EAST** Main cure: Earth Supported by: Fire Destroyed by: Wood	Career and Life Path **NORTH** Main cure: Water Supported by: Metal Destroyed by: Earth	Helpful Friends and Guides **NORTH-WEST** Main cure: Metal Supported by: Earth Destroyed by: Fire

Space-clearing with Crystals

Before you start making any Feng Shui adjustments to your home it is worth
cleansing the energy. You can use the methods of sound, smudge or incense
described under Cleansing Crystals (see pages 66–73) to clear your space. Choose
your favourite method and one that will be acceptable to the others who share
your home. Prepare yourself by making sure you are well grounded and have done
your protection. Set the intention that you will cleanse the energy in your home.
Walk around it methodically, paying particular attention to corners, where heavy
energy tends to accumulate.

Once you have cleansed each room in your home, you may feel a bit sticky or
heavy. If so, have a shower or a bath and change your clothes before moving on to
the next stage.

When you feel fresh and clean, choose a large clear quartz point and walk round
your home again. Hold the quartz in your hands and stand in the centre of each
room. Turn slowly clockwise, directing the point into the space, imagining white
light filling the room and bathing it from floor to ceiling.

Repeat the space-clearing following illness, after an argument or whenever you
sense it is needed.

Making Feng Shui Enhancements

It is advisable to make your Feng Shui enhancements gradually, room by room, and to monitor the effect. If you try to "Feng Shui" your home all at once, you may stir up too much energy and things can feel chaotic while it settles down again. You also won't know which of your crystal placements is working, and it will be harder to determine if any are not helpful. Looking at the Lo Shu Key, identify an aspect of your life that you would like to improve as a priority, then start with the corresponding area of your home.

Crystals are primarily Earth-element "cures" in Feng Shui. They are especially used to enhance the energy in Relationships and Marriage in the south-west and Education and Knowledge in the north-east. According to the Chinese five-element system, Earth supports Metal, so crystals can also be used to enhance Metal sectors. Metallic crystals such as haematite and pyrite are ideal for Children and Creativity in the west and Helpful Friends and Guides in the north-west. Crystals are considered unhelpful in the north, where the Water element is destroyed by Earth.

You may be drawn to make crystal placements around your home that don't correspond with the Lo Shu Key. Follow your intuition. Place the crystal in that area and see what the energy in the room feels like over the coming days. When you are arranging your crystals, be mindful that quartz will amplify the energy of whatever is around it. Make sure you are highlighting and amplifying the things you do want in your life and not drawing attention to things you don't want.

The Lo Shu Key may inspire you to rethink the use of rooms in your home. For example, if you have a guest bedroom in the south-west, you might want to claim it for yourself. Do what is most practical for you and your family. Very few homes have a perfect layout according to the Lo Shu Key, and making the space difficult to use would not be good Feng Shui.

Crystals in the Hallway

Your front door is the "mouth of chi", where energy enters your home. Make
sure your entrance is uncluttered and bright. Crystals placed near your front door
set the tone of the energy for your whole home and welcome you, your family
and your visitors each time you come in. What kind of atmosphere do you wish
to create?

Possible crystals include:
- Citrine for a happy and optimistic welcome
- Amethyst for a peaceful and spiritual vibe
- Rose quartz for a loving and harmonious atmosphere

The hallway is also a great place to locate a lucky-dip bag of assorted crystals
for you and your family to choose your crystal of the day before going out
into the world.

Crystals in the Living Room

In many households the living room is a multi-functional space. Think about the ways your living room gets used. Is it somewhere for watching TV, playing, relaxation, meditation; somewhere to entertain visitors, or a place to read? Use the main purpose of the room to guide your choice of crystals. For example, if your living room is a busy space where people gather to chat and socialize, you might want to place a clear quartz crystal cluster, which represents individuals living together harmoniously. If you use the space for yoga and meditation, an amethyst geode could set a spiritually uplifting ambience and create a peaceful sanctuary.

Crystals in the Kitchen

Kitchens are often the heart of the home where people like to gather, especially if there is a kitchen table to sit around. It makes sense to keep your kitchen work surfaces as clear as possible for food preparation, but crystals may find a safe niche on windowsills or shelves. Use crystals that are easy to wash in soapy water, as cooking can generate sticky and greasy residues. A crystal cluster on a kitchen windowsill sets a sociable vibe in a family kitchen or can become a table centrepiece, along with a candle, to create a convivial atmosphere at mealtimes.

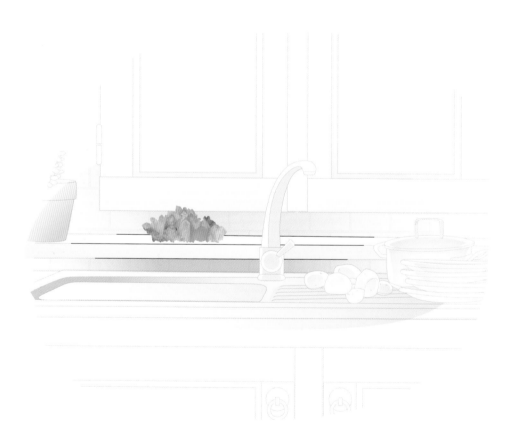

Making Gem Waters

You might like to place crystals in a jug to create gem water. Drinking water infused with a crystal is an easy way to absorb the crystal's energy throughout your body. Placing a water jug in the kitchen can encourage you and your loved ones to drink more water. If your tap water tastes unpleasant, try using a water-filter jug. Your body is approximately 60 per cent water, so drinking enough fluids is a key to good health. The exact amount of hydration you need each day depends on your size and how hot it is, but the general health recommendation for adults is around 1.2 litres (2 pints).

Make sure you choose non-toxic, non-soluble crystals for your water jug. Avoid any crystals that you suspect may have been dyed, or fragile crystals that could leave small fragments in the water. Tumblestones are a good choice for water jugs, and the quartz family is quite resilient and gives you a good range of options. If you have small children, keep the water jug out of their reach because crystals are a possible choking hazard.

Give your chosen crystals a good wash before you place them in the jug. Fill the jug with water and allow the crystalline energy some time to infuse the water. After an hour or two the gem water will be ready to drink. You can fill the jug last thing at night, so that the water is ready when you get up each morning.

Vary your choice of crystals for different effects:
- Clear quartz gem water helps you feel more awake and alert. A clear quartz tumblestone placed in the jug with any other crystal will amplify the energy of that crystal.
- Rose quartz gem water helps you feel more loving and more lovable.
- Citrine gem water helps to lift low moods and boost optimism.
- Smoky quartz gem water can assist a detox.
- Amethyst gem water can help you feel more peaceful.

Crystals in the Bathroom

The bathroom's function is primarily for cleansing. However, it can also become an oasis for self-care.

A crystal tealight holder in the bathroom helps to create a relaxing atmosphere for bathing and can turn the experience into a time for peaceful contemplation. You can place crystals in your bathwater to immerse yourself in their energy. Add your choice of non-toxic, non-soluble crystals to the bath for a crystalline bathing experience.

- Rose quartz can put you in the mood for love and romance
- Aquamarine is refreshing
- Amethyst helps you purify your energy and is relaxing before bedtime

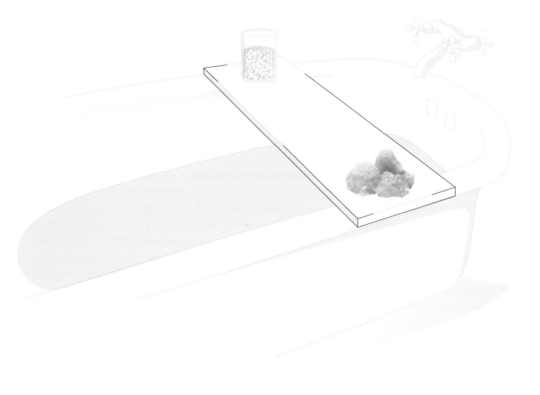

Crystals in the Bedroom

Your bedroom should be a peaceful and nurturing haven where you can relax and sleep. It may also be somewhere for love and romance. Make sure this is a place where you can switch off from the world. Phones, laptops and TVs bring a busy energy into the room, as well as emitting EMFs and blue light, which may disrupt deep, restorative sleep if used in the evenings or kept in the room overnight. Ideally, keep electronic devices out of your bedroom, but if you must have them there, switch them off overnight and place them as far from the bedside as possible.

Crystals for Sleep

Crystals that promote good sleep can be displayed beside the bed, or if they are flat and smooth they can be placed under the pillow.

- Lepidolite calms the mind. The raw form called a "lepidolite book" is particularly soothing when placed under the pillow.
- Howlite has a restful energy – use undyed white howlite.
- Celestite has a gentle but high vibration, which connects with the angelic realms. Place a celestite cluster by your bedside and ask the angels to watch over you as you sleep.
- Black obsidian can shield you as you sleep if you have disturbing dreams. Imagine climbing inside a sphere of black obsidian at bedtime.

You can grid your bed with crystals to create a haven for sleep. Use four protective or sleep-inducing crystals, and place one at each corner of your bed. Imagine they are joined with lines of crystalline light, then fill the space within the grid with pure, clean energy. Remember to cleanse these crystals periodically to keep the energy fresh.

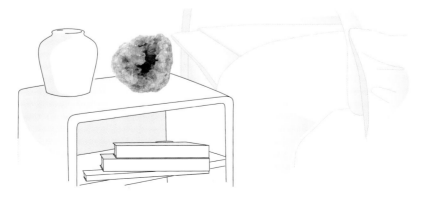

Crystal Dreaming

Your dreams can be a window into your subconscious mind and may offer you fascinating insights into your psyche. Dreams are usually symbolic and the interpretation of dream meanings can be an art. Sometimes they may make no sense, or will only make sense much later. Before you can start to decode your dreams, you need to remember them. You can train yourself to do this. Choose a notebook to be your dream journal and place it by your bedside with a pencil. You need to write your dreams down as soon as you wake, because the details quickly fade.

Select a crystal to be your ally for dream recall. Choose one that will fit under your pillow. It needs to have a peaceful energy, which aids sleep while promoting recollection. Cleanse the crystal. Now place it under your pillow at night, and in the morning reach for it and hold it as you write your dream journal. If your dream has grown hazy you can place your crystal on your third eye, where it may help you recall the images. Cleanse your dream crystal when you have finished your journal, then put it back under your pillow ready for the next night of dreaming. Charging your dream crystal once a month under the full moon will make it more receptive to your dream visions.

- Amethyst has a calming energy for the mind and may make your dreams more memorable
- Snow quartz has a more peaceful and receptive energy than clear quartz

Crystals for Love and Romance

The bedroom is the ideal place to put personal relationship crystals. If you are in a loving relationship, it can feel special to buy each other a relationship crystal as a gift. Choose meaningful crystals that symbolize love. Heart-shaped crystals are the obvious choice for love and relationships, but you might be drawn to something that feels more personalized.

Your two relationship crystals can be placed carefully together in a bowl surrounded by dried rose petals or pot-pourri. You can add some small rose quartz tumblestones to the dish. A few drops of essential oil can be added to dried flowers for fragrance, such as rose, geranium or ylang-ylang. Choose a scent you both enjoy. You might like to add a favourite photo of you both, and a candle and incense to create a romantic mood.

A Ritual for Self-worth

If you would like to find love, the first place to start is by loving yourself. By caring for yourself and appreciating your own qualities you emanate a positive energy that can attract a loving partner.

You will need:
- A journal and a pen
- A candle in a holder
- A piece of rose quartz or rhodocrosite
- A square of satin cloth
- A length of thin ribbon

1. Make a list in your journal of all your positive qualities. If your list isn't overly long, think about what your friends and colleagues say they like about you. Now is not a time for false modesty!

2. When you have written your list, light the candle and hold the crystal to your heart centre.

3. Look at the first quality on your list and say, "I am [name] and I am [quality]."

4. Pause and appreciate the feeling of really owning that positive quality.

5. Now look at the next quality on your list and say, "I am [name] and I am [quality]."

6. Pause again and let the good feelings build in you.

7. Keep repeating this simple formula until you have formally claimed all the positive qualities on your list.

8. Now place the crystal in the square of cloth and bring the corners together. Use the ribbon to tie the cloth just above the crystal, so that it is secured, then create a hanging loop from the rest of the ribbon. Hang the crystal on your bedpost or your dressing-table mirror.

9. Whenever you need to boost your self-worth, hold the crystal and remember your good qualities. If you feel the crystal needs cleansing, you can use smudge or incense so that you don't need to unwrap your crystal.

Children's Rooms

Crystals need to be kept out of reach of small children as they can be a choking hazard. Many children love crystals and may be eager to build a collection of their own. Give older children a place to display their crystals, if you have a budding crystal enthusiast.

Children are often highly intuitive and will make interesting choices of crystals. When you next have an ache or pain, ask your child to choose you a stone and see what they come up with. They may also want to place it on you. It's a therapeutic version of the popular Doctors and Nurses game.

For older children grow-your-own crystals kits are readily available. These can be a fun educational activity, used under supervision, and will teach the value of patience, because the crystals will take time to form. The crystals may look good, but they will be quite soft and fragile to handle.

Making a Crystal Dreamcatcher

Dreamcatchers are made by some Native American tribes. Help your child to sleep by creating a crystal dreamcatcher to hang over the bed. Explain to the child that the dreamcatcher will capture any horrid dreams, so that they only have nice ones.

You will need:

- A hoop (craft suppliers sell hoops, or you can make one out of a flexible piece of willow by binding the two ends together; this will be teardrop-shaped rather than round and will give the dreamcatcher a more natural and rustic look)
- A ribbon or leather thong in your child's favourite colour
- Glue
- Strong thread or yarn (natural or coloured)
- Crystal beads (include some made from protective or peaceful stones, such as smoky quartz, amethyst or howlite; turquoise is a good choice if you want to connect with Native American tradition)
- Clean feathers (either found or bought from craft stores; gently wash feathers that you find in mild detergent and let them air-dry)

1. Begin by wrapping the hoop. Tie one end of the ribbon or thong to the hoop and then wrap it round, keeping the tension firm and using a spot of glue every few wraps to keep it from unravelling. Tie off the end when you get all the way round the hoop. Let the glue dry.

2. Take the thread or yarn and tie one end to the hoop. Bring it a few centimetres (inches) along the perimeter and keep it taut as you pass it through the loop you have made, so that it holds firm. Repeat the process, turning the hoop clockwise until you have worked all the way round to your starting point.

3. Moving the hoop clockwise, this time pass your thread around the midpoint of the first loop you made, keeping the tension. Continue moving the hoop clockwise as you weave. You can add crystal beads every few loops as you work. You'll be weaving your way toward the centre. Keep adding beads and weaving until you get to the middle and then tie off the thread.

4. Now make some tassels to tie to the bottom of the dreamcatcher. An odd number such as three or five looks most effective. Tie a few feathers together to make the bottom of the tassel and then add some crystal beads. Knot the tassels to the bottom of your dreamcatcher, with the longest one in the middle.

5. Once completed, you may want to smudge the dreamcatcher, then it is ready to hang above your child's bed.

Crystals in the Garden

Most crystals enjoy being outside in the elements. You just need to be careful with those that fade over time in sunlight, such as amethyst and fluorite, and those that are water-sensitive. You can create a space for peaceful contemplation in your garden with the help of your crystals. Choose a quiet corner where you are not overlooked and can sit and relax. Find a flat surface for your altar and add objects that represent the elements. Include a dish for water, a lantern for a candle and a holder for incense. Add an altar crystal. This outdoor space can be a more natural and rustic alternative to making an indoor altar, and can be a place for you to meditate, dedicate your crystals and charge them.

Most plants enjoy the company of crystals, and you can place them in plant pots indoors or outdoors. Retiring a broken crystal to a plant pot is an alternative to burying it in the earth.

Birthstones

Ayurvedic astrology has a long and venerable history of ascribing gems to the planets. There is also evidence dating back to the 1st century CE that the 12 gemstones on the breastplate of the high priest described in the book of Exodus had been assigned astrological associations. Different lists of stones for the months are available, ranging from the Jewish list – which is probably the first and reflects the stones of the breastplate – to Roman and Arabian lists. The custom of wearing a birthstone associated with your month of birth seems to have begun relatively recently in Poland, in the 18th century. Prior to that, it is thought that some people would have a collection of 12 stones and would carry the one that was associated with the calendar month.

In 1912 a modern list of birthstones was created by the National Association of Jewellers. Their list is the one most frequently cited today, but it must be remembered that their primary motivation was commercial; they wanted to sell more gemstone jewellery.

The selection given here is made from both the modern and traditional lists, to suit the characteristics of each zodiac sign. As the birthstones were traditionally assigned to the month of birth, and zodiac dates flow across two months, you may feel more drawn to a birthstone associated with the signs on either side of your own.

Your zodiac sign indicates where the Sun was placed in the zodiac when you were born. Most people know their Sun sign and are familiar with its key attributes from their horoscopes. It is important to realize that the position of the Sun is only one aspect of your personal horoscope, and therefore it only paints your personality with broad brushstrokes. You are more than your Sun sign, so if you don't resonate with the general characteristics of it, you may wish to look at your birth chart to see where other planetary influences were at the time of your birth.

Aries (21 March–20 April)

Aries comes at the start of the zodiac and is ruled by the planet
Mars and the element of Fire. Aries people have a need to be seen,
heard and recognized; they can be excellent champions for good
causes. These are busy, driven people who are goal-oriented and
can be adventurous. They may find inactivity hard to cope with
and can be impatient or attention-seeking.

Bloodstone

Diamond is a modern choice of birthstone for Aries. Its
adamantine (brilliant) shine and sparkling nature can support
the focus and determination that those born under Aries need
in order to pursue their goals.

A more traditional birthstone for Aries is bloodstone, the stone
of courage, with long association of use by warriors.

Note: Many sources assign aquamarine to Aries, but the watery
aspect of the stone can put out the Aries fire. Aquamarine is better
suited to those with earlier March birthdays falling under Pisces.

Taurus (21 April–20 May)

Taureans are practical and reliable types. These are the people to
turn to for help and advice. As they are ruled by the beautiful
planet Venus, they do best when in stable, loving relationships.
As an Earth sign, they are normally well grounded. Taureans can
be rather stubborn and fixed in their thinking.

Sapphire

Sapphire is traditionally assigned to Taureans born in April and
supports the honesty of their personality.

Agate is a traditional birthstone choice for May, which suits
Taurus's down-to-earth nature.

Gemini (21 May–20 June)

Quick-witted Geminis are the tricksters of the zodiac. Like all the Air signs, they are thinkers. They tend to have a lively intelligence and a good sense of fun. Their ruling planet is Mercury, which is so fast-moving it lends its name to the description "mercurial", which describes the Gemini personality well. Their symbol is the twins, and Geminis tend to have pronounced light and dark sides to their persona. When the light twin is around, they are fun, but watch out when the dark twin takes the lead! Geminis need stimulation and change and are easily bored.

Emerald

Emerald is supportive for Gemini; it is the modern gemstone assigned to May and the traditional choice for June. As a stone of balance, it can bring harmony to the Gemini persona.

Carnelian is an alternative for Gemini, which relates to the earliest list based on the high priest's breastplate. It helps to ground the airy nature of the sign so that the Gemini can put plans into practice.

Cancer (21 June–22 July)

Cancerians are usually highly psychic, artistic and imaginative. They tend to put a protective shell around themselves to avoid being overwhelmed, like the crab that is their symbol. They need to feel safe and secure, so home is particularly important to them. As a Water-element sign, they are more sensitive and emotional than most. Being ruled by the Moon can make their moods changeable.

Moonstone

Pearl is an appropriate choice for Cancerians. It is an organic gem formed by an oyster and so has an affinity to water. The Moon controls the tides, and pearls are products of the sea; they also have a sheen that resembles the Moon. Some believe that "seeding" pearls in oysters to culture them and harvesting them is cruel.

Moonstone is an ethical alternative for Cancerians. It has a receptive lunar nature, softens extremes and helps the emotions flow.

Leo (23 July–22 August)

Leos have a regal air about them, being endowed with ample self-belief and an expectation that they will command respect and adulation. They are ruled by the Sun and are a Fire-element sign. They can draw people to them with their warm, magnanimous characters. It makes Leos happy to be in charge and to know that they have authority. To be answerable to others does not suit them, and if their authority is challenged or they feel humiliated, they can be angered.

Ruby

Ruby is a suitable gemstone for Leos. It has a long history of being chosen for Crown Jewels and a strong affinity with the Sun. Ruby supports the strength and stamina needed to be in charge.

Onyx is a traditional choice of birthstone for Leos. It helps to create strong boundaries.

Virgo (23 August–22 September)

Virgo is renowned as a star sign of beauty, symbolized by the maiden. As an Earth-element sign, Virgoans like to collect things and tend look after, organize and display their possessions well. They like everything in life to be well ordered. Their perfectionist tendencies can get in the way of accomplishing all they are capable of, and their high expectations of others means they are often disappointed by human nature. Perfectionism makes them likely to be self-critical and find fault in others. Virgo is ruled by Mercury, but the Earth element gives them more stability than their fellow Mercurians, Gemini.

Peridot

Blue sapphire is often recommended as a birthstone for Virgo to support their love of truth and authenticity.

Peridot's bright energy is a traditional choice for September and suits beauty-loving Virgoans. It has an optimistic and cheering energy that lifts the spirits.

Libra (23 September–22 October)

Like the scales that symbolize their star sign, Librans like balance. They are probably the most peace-loving star sign and are most happy when they are surrounded by harmony. As an Air sign, they think deeply. Librans like to weigh things up carefully and make their decisions with care. It can be stressful for a Libran to be put on the spot or rushed into making a choice. They find arguments and disputes distressing and can be over-sensitive to slight where none was intended.

Morganite

Aquamarine is the traditional choice for October, but beryl appears on some lists, giving Librans several options. Morganite would suit the Libran love of harmony.

Opals are a more modern choice of birthstone for Librans.

Scorpio (23 October–22 November)

Those born under Scorpio are often intuitive and psychic. The Water element in their sign makes them sensitive to energy. Scorpios are known for being sensual, brooding and mysterious. They can be serious in outlook and may have the most intense personalities of any star sign. Their symbol is the scorpion and that gives fair warning to avoid pushing Scorpio too far; if they are angered, you may feel the sting in their tail.

Golden topaz

Golden topaz is a good choice for Scorpios, helping them develop mastery of their chosen profession or pastime.

Amethyst makes a good alternative, assisting Scorpios with their psychic gifts while having a calming effect on the temper.

Sagittarius (23 November–21 December)

The Sagittarian personality is interested in ideas, discussion and debate. The Fire element in this sign makes for a warm personality, but Sagittarians can be argumentative just for the joy of sparring. Their ruling planet is Jupiter, which encourages expansion and optimism. Like the archer that is their symbol, when they set their sights on a target Sagittarians follow through to achieve their ambitions. They are adventurous and like to travel and explore. This trait can make them restless; settling down may be a challenge.

Blue topaz

Blue topaz helps Sagittarians express themselves with clarity.

Golden topaz strengthens the will and supports the Sagittarian's ambitious nature.

Capricorn (22 December–19 January)

Capricorn is an Earth sign and shares the trait of stability and trustworthiness with others. Capricorns are diligent and hard-working and know the meaning of commitment. Most will enjoy research, so academic studies usually suit the Capricorn personality. Their ruling planet of Saturn can be a hard taskmaster, and sometimes Capricorns can become too serious and blinkered, needing to take time out and have some fun.

Turquoise

Ruby is the historical choice for Capricorn, as a warming and strengthening gemstone that supports wellbeing in midwinter. It matches the stability and steadfastness of the Capricorn personality.

Turquoise is also listed as a choice for December birthdays. It is a more modern association, perhaps because turquoise helps to gather and centre energy, which provides stamina to get through the colder months.

Aquarius (20 January–18 February)

Aquarians are the visionaries of the zodiac, ruled by Uranus, which drives their tendency to rebel and instigate change. They love to see the big picture and get excited by new opportunities and good causes. As an Air sign, they have plenty of ideas – perhaps too many to put into action. Aquarians may have strong leadership qualities, but may also be quite detached emotionally, and unavailable in their personal relationships. They can be too absorbed in their latest cause to pay attention to what their loved ones need.

Garnet

Garnet is the primary birthstone for Aquarians. It helps to ground some of their big ideas so that they can make them happen. Garnet also supports the stamina and commitment required to see plans through.

Zircon is another warming red stone, which used to be called jacinth and is believed to have been one of the stones of the high priest's breastplate.

Pisces (19 February–20 March)

Pisceans are the mature souls of the zodiac, born at the end of the cycle. They tend to feel everything deeply. With Water as their element and Neptune as their ruling planet, they are sensitive and are often interested in mysticism. Their symbol of two fishes underlines their watery nature. Pisceans are often psychic and intuitive. They are happiest living a peaceful life where they can give their imagination and artistic abilities free rein. They don't like conflict, and find arguments stressful.

Amethyst

Amethyst resonates with the mystical soul and is the crystal most often assigned for Pisces. It promotes a peaceful outlook and releases tension.

Aquamarine is suggested for Pisceans with March birthdays. Its refreshing nature and association with the sea suit the watery nature of the birth sign.

7

BUYER'S GUIDE

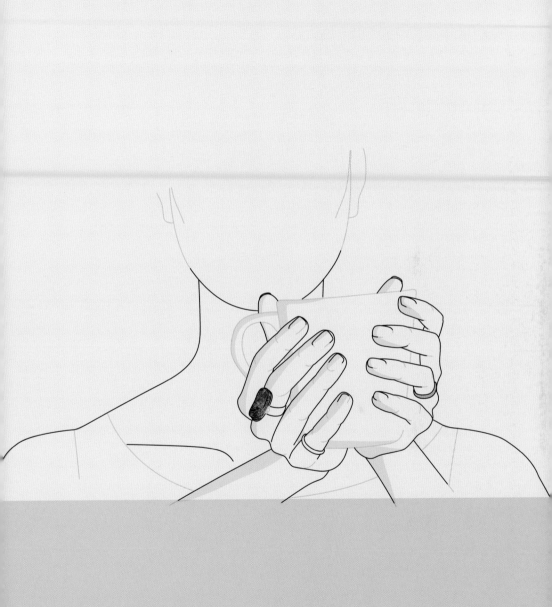

Buying Your Crystals

When you discover the beautiful world of crystals you are likely to build your collection quickly. Crystals are moreish! Looking at the brightly coloured crystals arranged for sale can transport you back to childhood memories of visiting a favourite sweet shop.

Follow your instincts and intuition when buying crystals. Go shopping on a day when you feel alert, and do your grounding and protection before you head out. Purchasing your crystals in person is preferable, if possible. If you feel drawn to a crystal, pick it up to test if its energy feels good to you. Out of courtesy, do check with the seller before you start touching their crystals.

Larger shops and gem shows can feel overwhelming, with thousands of crystals to choose from. It may be useful to prepare a wishlist to keep your mind focused. Be aware that crystals are natural products and their supply isn't necessarily constant, so you may not be able to source everything on your list. If you are looking for a specific type of crystal but can't see it, don't be afraid to ask. Specialist crystal shops often have more stock than they can display and may have the crystal you want tucked away.

Although large crystals may be eye-catching and look more impressive, you will sometimes experience more healing energy from a smaller crystal. The quality of the stone and its resonance with you are more important than size. A high-quality example can outshine a lower-quality piece several times its size.

If you are lucky enough to have a crystal shop in your neighbourhood, it is great to visit regularly to buy a few crystals at a time. By adding to your collection slowly you'll have the opportunity to become more familiar with the crystals individually. You'll also get to know your local crystal shopkeeper and will probably have some interesting discussions.

Sometimes the crystals you are drawn to are priced out of your budget, and it can be difficult to leave a fabulous crystal behind in a shop. It may feel like the crystal is calling to you. Individual crystals can play on your mind for weeks or even months afterwards. If this happens, it is usually a sign that you and the crystal have some work to do together. Start saving up and contact the shop to check whether that crystal is still in stock.

If you visit a gem show, it is a good idea to have a walk around first and see what catches your eye before you start buying. Sometimes several stallholders are selling similar crystals and one seller may have better prices, or better-quality merchandise, than the others. Although most sellers at shows are not crystal healers, a lot of them are extremely knowledgeable about their crystals and will be able to give you background information, including where their crystals come from. Some stallholders travel overseas and buy their stock direct from the mines.

New Age shops almost always have a crystal section, and Mind Body Spirit fairs usually have a few crystal sellers. Sometimes you can spot lovely crystals in unexpected places, such as craft markets, museum gift shops or other tourist attractions. It is worth keeping your eyes open.

Buying Crystals Online

If you don't have a crystal shop nearby or any shows to visit, you'll need to buy your crystals online. This can be successful if you purchase with care. Many online retailers just display a picture of a sample crystal from their stock. That may be sufficient for cheap tumblestones, but when you are paying more for a specimen crystal you'll want to see the actual piece you are purchasing.

The best online sellers take time to photograph the individual crystals, often from several angles. They will also give a clear write-up. If there is a photo of the crystal you are interested in purchasing, you can tune into the crystal. Prepare your energy by grounding and protecting in the same way as you would to choose a crystal in person. Focus on the image of the crystal and then pendulum dowse or intuit whether it is the right one for you.

It is probably safest to avoid buying on generic marketplace sites, as there is a huge variety of sellers and it is extremely easy to make mistakes. A lot of fake and misleadingly labelled stones make their way onto these marketplaces. This shouldn't be a problem if you know a reputable seller who trades on one of these sites. If you are tempted to buy online from an unknown seller, check their returns policy and look carefully at their customer reviews or feedback scores. When you purchase from suppliers abroad, you will usually be liable for all the import taxes. Thresholds are set for duty, so do your research carefully to avoid a surprise bill, which can make your crystal bargain rather expensive.

Buying Crystals on Holiday

Bringing home crystals from your holiday can conjure up good memories for years to come. Holding a crystal from a holiday destination can take you straight back to the experience and evoke the sights, sounds and smells of the land.

Crystals sold on street stalls in the countries where they are mined are usually considerably cheaper than they would be at home in the shops. Do buy with care, as your normal consumer rights are unlikely to apply; and haggle on price, if that is the local custom.

Remember that rocks can be heavy in your suitcase. Check your weight allowance, because paying for excess baggage can get expensive. Wrap any purchases carefully. Many crystals are easily damaged, and luggage can be treated roughly. Wrapping the crystals in your clothes can protect them. You may find that your suitcase gets opened by airport security, as crystals show up as strange solid shapes on airport X-ray machines.

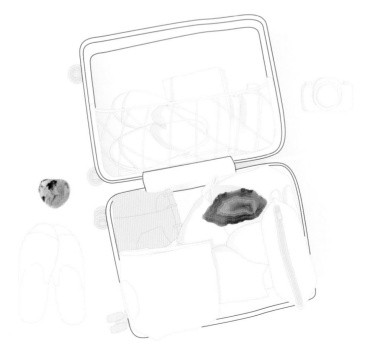

Commonly Substituted Crystals

Gemstones can be expensive and there is a long history of using other, cheaper crystals to substitute for a costly stone. The trade in crystals is not as tightly regulated as some products, so *caveat emptor* – buyer beware – applies. If you are buying from a specialist crystal shop, then any dyed or man-made stones should normally be labelled as such and fakes shouldn't be an issue, although other crystal sellers may not be so well informed.

Typically, the more expensive the crystal, the more careful you need to be. After all, there isn't much profit to be made from substituting a cheap stone. An example of this is turquoise, which is often mimicked with dyed blue howlite; if this is sold responsibly, it will be given the trade name of "turquenite". Diamonds can be substituted with cubic zirconia, which is a man-made crystal. Reputable sellers will clearly label these as such and sell them for a fraction of the price of real diamonds.

Probably the most misleading fakery of recent years concerns moldavite. Glass is being manufactured to look like moldavite, and the market has been flooded with imitation pieces. Sometimes they are even sold in display boxes, with information about the meteorite impact they supposedly came from. These deliberate fakes are designed to fool crystal enthusiasts and are often sold for high prices. Unfortunately the differences between real moldavite (being a natural glass) and fake moldavite (also glass) can be hard to spot visually. Moldavite is becoming increasingly rare, and genuine large pieces are hard to source. If you are buying in person you can ask to hold the moldavite in your hand. With real moldavite, most people can detect a little tingle in their palm or may have a stronger reaction. You are unlikely to feel much from fake moldavite. Be cautious about purchasing moldavite online unless it is coming from a reputable source.

Man-made Stones

There are a lot of man-made stones on the market, and often these are cheap and made of glass. Their bright colours can be eye-catching. Sometimes trade names used for them are deceptive, and purchasers may assume they are buying a real crystal. Blue obsidian is a common example. It is a manufactured transparent blue glass. Cherry quartz is also clear glass with attractive red threads running through it. Perhaps the most confusing man-made stone is goldstone, which is brown glass with copper glitter. It has been made since the 18th century and is popular because it is so pretty. It is frequently used in jewellery, as well as being available as tumblestones and palm stones (see page 167). Blue goldstone is a deep-blue version.

Cat's-eye crystals show chatoyancy, which is a shine rather like a cat's eye. When this phenomenon occurs naturally, the crystals are usually cut and polished *en cabochon* (with a convex dome shape) to display the effect and are highly sought-after. There is a manufactured cat's-eye that shows a similar chatoyancy, due to fibre-optics. Synthetic cat's-eye is often dyed in lurid colours and is cheap to purchase.

Laboratory-grown versions of many gemstones are available, including emeralds, rubies and diamonds. They are grown under controlled conditions and are perfect, containing no inclusions (other material trapped within the crystal), which makes them more desirable for industrial uses, such as the synthetic rubies that are used in lasers. Lab-grown gems are sometimes used in jewellery, but reputable retailers should make this clear. Physically the gemstone should be nature-identical, although most crystal enthusiasts prefer their gemstones to have grown over a long period of time in the Earth with their inclusions, rather than perfectly over weeks or months in a laboratory.

Sometimes lab-grown crystals are more attractive than the natural crystal to look at. For example, natural bismuth is a dull grey metal, but when it is melted and grown in the laboratory it can re-form in geometric shapes, which look like otherworldly stepped pyramids and show iridescent rainbow hues. These pieces can be very attractive. They are real crystals, even though they did not form in the Earth. It is a matter of personal taste whether you include lab-grown crystals in your collection.

Enhanced and Man-altered Crystals

Many crystals are routinely heat-treated to improve their colour, especially those gem-quality stones that are cut for jewellery, including rubies, sapphires and blue topaz. This treatment can enhance their clarity too. Emeralds are normally oiled to improve their appearance. These crystals will rarely be labelled as treated, because these enhancements have become the industry standard.

Sometimes heat-treatments change the look and feel of the crystal more radically. Amethyst is regularly heat-treated. The purple colour changes and becomes yellow, orange or brown. If these crystals were labelled with their correct name – burnt amethyst – it would be less misleading than selling them as citrine, which is the norm. Burnt amethyst does not look, or feel, the same as natural citrine. It is still a crystal, however, so if you have a piece and you like it, there is no reason to stop using it.

Crackle quartz is clear quartz that has been heated and then rapidly cooled, creating stress-fractures inside, which gives it a crackled effect and makes it sparkle with internal light. An alternative trade name for clear quartz points treated in this way is "fire and ice" quartz. Crackle quartz may be dyed a range of colours. A lot of people find these crystals attractive, although creating internal fractures does weaken them and makes them more prone to breakage. Some people feel the process of thermally shocking a crystal to create internal fractures is too harsh and may be traumatic for the crystal.

Agates are commonly dyed, often with bright colours to suit the gift trade. Underneath the colour, they are still real crystals. It is up to you whether you purchase them, but most collectors prefer the earthy brown tones of natural agate.

A few man-made enhancements are expensive and add value to the crystal. Precious metals are vaporized and bonded with clear quartz in a vacuum chamber to create aura quartzes. The bond is permanent and will not peel away or wash off. The results of this specialized process are visually beautiful, and many healers report that the fusion of precious metal with quartz creates a special alchemy, resulting in high-vibrational crystals.

There are many aura quartz varieties now available, with more being created as the makers experiment. Some popular varieties include aqua aura, which is created using gold vapour that turns the quartz an eye-catching blue colour. Angel aura quartz is made using silver and platinum vapour, creating an ethereal colour-changing iridescence. Ruby aura quartz is made with gold and silver vapours; best-quality pieces are a deep ruby-red. Flame aura quartz is bonded with cobalt, producing a deep-blue crystal with an iridescent shine. A similar process is used for clear topaz, which is bonded with titanium to create mystic topaz.

Mystic topaz

Crackle quartz

Angel aura quartz

Aqua aura quartz

Ethical Purchasing

Consumers have become more aware of environmental concerns and workers' welfare in the last few decades. Fairtrade foods and clothing are accessible, but Fairtrade certification doesn't yet cover crystals. If you are concerned about the environment and workers' rights there are some ways to purchase your crystals as ethically as possible.

A simple method to keep the carbon footprint of your crystal collection low is to buy those crystals that are mined in your own country. They haven't travelled far to get to you. You can also have reasonable confidence that the working conditions are well regulated, if you are in a country with strong health-and-safety legislation. This buying approach limits your choice of crystals, but it can be very nurturing and grounding to work with native crystals. You may be able to visit the areas they come from and connect with the energy of the land. If you would like more choice, you might extend your purchasing to crystals that come from other countries with similar health-and-safety standards.

Much of the mining in the developing world is small-scale. This is called artisanal mining and it is estimated that 80 per cent of gemstones are sourced in this way. The miners are often subsistence workers who rely on their trade for their livelihood. If crystals were no longer purchased from artisanal mines it would cause great hardship. This does not overlook the need for safer working conditions and fairer prices for artisanal miners. There are signs that the industry is beginning to take the issues surrounding mining seriously. Some crystal suppliers visit the mines in person and check on working conditions for themselves, and you may find out more by having a chat with the retailer. However, most shops are reliant on background information provided by wholesalers, which is often very basic.

Carved crystals raise another issue regarding workers' rights and health and safety. A lot of crystals are mined and then shipped to countries with low wages, such as China or India, to be worked. In some areas of the world it is still considered acceptable to use child labour. Conditions for workers in factories are sometimes unsafe – for example, proper face masks are not always provided for those who carve quartz. Breathing in silica dust is damaging to the lungs and can lead to the serious respiratory condition called silicosis. It is hard to know for certain what the conditions are like, unless the supplier has visited the factory. If you want to be sure that you are not contributing to potential health issues and the exploitation of workers, you may wish to avoid buying shaped or carved crystals; or you could buy them from producers in your own country.

Avoiding the purchase of crystals from war-torn areas of the globe is probably the safest way to ensure your money is not going toward funding more fighting. The political situation is constantly changing, so if this is a concern for you, then you will need to stay up to date with world events. Some of the most unstable countries also use slave labour.

Although some sectors of the media have spoken about crystals as if mining them creates environmental devastation, the disruption caused by mining crystals is mostly small-scale. The most obvious exception is that of large diamond mines, where deep pits are dug with heavy machinery to extract the gemstones. The environmental impact of mining crystals is not to be ignored, and asking questions about where and how your crystals were sourced puts healthy pressure on the trade in crystals to become more ethical.

The level of environmental disruption caused by mining for crystals is far less extreme than the huge mining and quarrying operations of industry, or the large-scale deforestation of the rainforests caused by the demand for palm oil used in convenience foods. Everything is relative.

Storing and Transporting Your Crystals Safely

Crystals can be delicate and a real investment. It makes sense to think about how you will organize and store your collection to keep them in the best possible condition.

Tumblestones are relatively robust. If you would like to carry your crystals about with you, then these are the most practical choice. Take note of their hardness on Mohs Scale (see page 28) because, even when tumbled, the softer stones can scratch. It is a good idea to have a soft pouch to protect your crystals if you are putting them in your pocket, especially if they are sharing it with car keys or coins. A fabric or leather pouch will not prevent the healing energy of the crystal reaching you. If you need to transport more delicate crystals, make sure they are well protected with bubblewrap or layers of tissue.

If you want to carry a collection of crystals around, look for a segmented container so that they don't bash against each other. Craft shops often have boxes and bags with lots of small sections and these can work well. You can also look out for other containers that can be repurposed, such as make-up caddies or jewellery boxes. If you line the segmented sections with fabric it will give the crystals extra protection.

Displaying your crystal collection on shelves or in a cabinet can look great. Tumblestones can be placed together in bowls, if you handle them gently and are mindful of the softer crystals. Arranging crystals by colour can make finding the one you want easier.

Open shelves make choosing crystals easy, but they can get dusty. A cabinet looks smart and is a good way to keep your crystals safe if you have pets or small children. Collectors' cabinets and other small drawers and boxes are great for keeping your crystals protected and dust-free, but they make choosing more difficult, because you can't see your crystals as easily.

Does the Shape Matter?

Crystals are available in a whole range of shapes and forms, some natural and some carved. Does the shape matter? Natural shapes can affect the way energy moves through and around the crystal. Carved shapes may influence the way the energy moves, depending on the shape and skill with which they have been carved. Some carving is done more for aesthetic than healing purposes, but the best carvings will be made with sympathy for the crystal.

Crystal Points

Naturally terminated crystals are often found in the quartz family. Energy will flow in the direction of the point. If you want to receive healing energy from a crystal point, direct it toward your body; if you want to release old energies, then direct it away from you. Other crystals that form natural terminations may be used to direct energy in the same way. Examples include tourmaline and danburite.

Clear quartz points are sometimes polished and cut to give them a flat base, enabling them to stand upright. These standing points can provide a powerful focus to collect and send energy when placed in the centre of a healing grid, or they may simply look beautiful in the home.

Microcrystalline members of the quartz family are normally found in massive form, meaning that they form as chunks without any natural points. Where natural points exist, these tend to be tiny. Examples include rose quartz, aventurine and tiger's eye. If you see these crystals as points, they will have been carved into the shape. Carving a point doesn't necessarily mean the energy of the crystal will move in the direction of the point.

Point

Geodes

A geode is a cavity within a rock in which crystals have grown. Unless they have been opened, the crystals cannot be seen. Small geodes lined with quartz crystals can be brought whole, to be cracked open at home, which can be exciting for older children. Celestite is also found as geodes. Amethyst geodes are usually cut cleanly in half to reveal the crystals inside. Larger pieces are sometimes called amethyst "churches" or "cathedrals". Geodes can set a beautiful energy in a room and are ideal for placing in a meditation or healing space. The yellow-brown geodes sold as citrine are heat-treated amethyst.

Large amethyst geodes are extremely heavy to move. Regular cleansing using an essence spray, incense, smudge or sound is easier than washing them. If a geode is physically dirty, pick it up carefully – with assistance if necessary – and take it to the garden and use a gentle garden spray to cleanse it with water. Alternatively, take it to the shower, but place a towel underneath so that it doesn't scratch the shower tray. Use the shower head on a gentle setting to wash the geode.

Geode

Clusters and Beds

Quartz crystals may grow together as a cluster, and amethyst beds of crystals are also available. Clusters of crystals symbolize the potential to live alongside each other in peace and harmony. As well as being beautiful additions to a room, they can be useful for resting and recharging other crystals. You'll need to keep your cluster cleansed and charged to use them in this way.

Blades

Some crystals form natural blades. Bladed crystals such as kyanite can be used for cutting away stagnant energies and clearing away unhealthy energy cords. They are not used for cutting anything physical.

Cluster

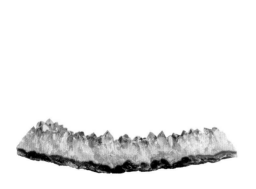

Bed

Blade

Tumblestones

The crystal tumbling process involves rolling raw chunks of crystals in different grades of grit, from coarse to fine. This process takes off rough edges and creates a smooth shape with a polished appearance. Some crystals such as malachite are more aesthetically pleasing once they have been polished, as their patterns can be fully appreciated.

Tumblestones are generally a bit more robust than the crystals in their raw form. They are a practical choice if you want to carry crystals around with you. You still need to treat them with care, however, as they are not indestructible. Softer tumbled stones can be scratched; and those such as calcite or celestite may cleave, or split, if dropped, showing a flat plane that reveals their underlying crystalline structure.

Tumblestones often form the foundation of a new collection because they are readily available, and generally more affordable than specimen crystals. They come in a wide range of types. Size varies from tiny crystals, like fish-tank gravel, to large tumblestones that fill the palm of the hand. In healing, a tumblestone tends to have a softer, more diffuse energy than its raw counterpart as it has literally had its edges taken off.

Palm Stones

Crystals carved into palm stones are usually oval, slim and smooth on each side. They fit nicely in the hand and are a comforting shape to hold. Palm stones also have the advantage of a relatively flat shape, which means they can be easily placed on the body without rolling off. They are carved from a wide variety of crystals and are a good practical shape to carry around with you, slipping neatly into a pocket or purse.

Tumblestone

Palm stone

Spheres

Spheres are symbolic of wholeness, or oneness. Some crystals form naturally in a spherical shape, such as nodules of azurite, but the vast majority of crystal spheres will have been carved. Spheres are available in a variety of crystals and a range of sizes and look beautiful on display. Make sure you place them on a secure stand so that they don't roll and get damaged. They tend to be more expensive by weight than the same crystal in its raw form. As well as the time taken to create a sphere, a large amount of crystal has to be lost to carve the shape.

Clear quartz crystal spheres conjure up images of fortune-tellers, and they can be used for scrying. Gazing into a crystal sphere can send the mind into an altered state. In this state, images and impressions may appear. If you use a sphere for scrying it is traditional to keep it covered between uses with a black silk cloth. You may wish to charge your scrying sphere under a full moon, as this is believed to enhance the psychic receptivity of the crystal.

In a healing context a sphere radiates energy smoothly all around it, and this can be a harmonious way to work with the crystal energy. Spheres can be used to give a massage by rolling them gently around the skin.

Eggs

Crystals carved into egg shapes have a similar smooth energy to spheres. Additionally the egg shape is symbolic of new beginnings, fertility, new life and spring, so you may like to meditate with one, especially when you have a creative project about to start, or when you welcome a new addition to your family. Crystal eggs make a lovely alternative gift to chocolate at Easter.

Sphere

Egg

Cubes

Some crystals, such as pyrite and fluorite, may form natural cubes. Cubes represent solidity and stability. They resonate most with the base chakra. Holding a crystal cube at a time of change, or when you feel anxious, can help to stabilize and ground your energy.

Hearts

Heart-shaped crystals symbolize love and romance. Many types of crystals can be found carved into hearts. They are most popular carved from rose quartz. Placing heart-shaped crystals on and around your body in healing can reinforce the intention that you are nurturing yourself. Heart-shaped crystals can be a lovely gift to show you care for someone. In the home a heart-shaped crystal placed on the bedside table can symbolize your readiness for love and romance.

Massage Wands

Massage wands are carved from a variety of crystals. Some are rounded at both ends, others rounded at one end and pointed at the other. The rounded ends of massage wands have a smooth energy. If you have achy joints, try using a massage wand gently in small anticlockwise circles to release congested energy.

If the massage wand has a point at one end, it may move the energy in a more directional way, although this effect is not as pronounced as for natural crystal points. After releasing congested energy you can cleanse the wand and turn it round, to use the point to put fresh energy into the area you worked on. Keep the point raised a few centimetres (inches) off the skin and move it clockwise for best results.

Cube

Heart

Massage wand

Skulls

Carved crystal skulls are the Marmite of the crystal world, dividing crystal enthusiasts equally between attraction and repulsion. If you are drawn to a crystal skull, then you may find it is an ally in contemplating mortality and the transience of all physical life. The popularity of crystal skulls is based on legends about ancient ones. Some of these skulls are famous, such as the Mitchell-Hedges skull and the one on display in London's British Museum. The antiquity of the Mitchell-Hedges skull is questionable; however, many people feel that crystal skulls are powerful objects. There is a huge range of quality in commercially available crystal skulls, from those mass-produced in their thousands, to exceptional artisan-carved skulls. Skull enthusiasts often use their crystal skulls to channel information. Take particular care with your energy safety, if this is something you are interested in trying.

Pyramids

There has been a resurgence of interest in Ancient Egypt and the iconic pyramid shape, and crystals carved into pyramids are available. There is no evidence that the Egyptians used carved pyramids in their healing, but the pyramids are believed to have been used as initiation chambers and were aligned with the stars. You may want to experiment with using a pyramid-shaped crystal at your third eye or crown chakra in meditation. Natural pyramidal crystals of apophyllite are available.

Skull

Pyramid

Octahedrons

Fluorite can cleave into octahedron-shaped (eight-faced) crystals. The octahedron shape looks like two pyramids stuck together, base to base. Sometimes crystals are carved into this shape. Looked at when balanced on a point, the shape combines an upward-pointing, masculine pyramid directed to the heavens, and a downward-pointing, feminine pyramid pointing to the Earth. This is a shape of perfect balance and it can help us rebalance our own masculine and feminine energies, as well as reminding us that we should keep our energies balanced between Heaven and Earth.

Merkabah Stars

The Merkabah is a complex shape. Imagine taking the Seal of Solomon (see page 126), making the two triangles into three-dimensional tetrahedra (geometric shapes with four faces), merging them and then giving one a twist, so that the points are arranged equally. Like the octahedron, the Merkabah unites Heaven and Earth and masculine and feminine energies. Some believe it to be the geometric shape of the light body in which the soul can travel between dimensions. Mer-ka-ba translates as "light, spirit, body".

Octahedron

Merkabah star

8
CRYSTAL
DIRECTORY

Agate

Keyword: Understanding
Affirmation: I develop a clearer understanding of the issues in my life
Chakras: Brow, throat, solar plexus, sacral, base
Chemical formula: SiO_2
Hardness: 7

Rough fire agate

Tumbled blue-lace agate

Banded agate slice

Tumbled moss agate

DID YOU KNOW?
The name "agate" comes from the Achates river in Sicily, where agates were found at least 3,000 years ago. Because of its eye-like banded patterns, it was believed agate could turn away the evil eye. Agate beads were produced in large numbers for protection.

Tumbled tree agate

Agates are a form of chalcedony, which is part of the quartz family. There is a wide variety of agate available and most types have a calming energy.

Banded agates, such as Botswana agate, can be helpful for working through the layers of an issue. Their earthy tones make them gently grounding.

Blue-lace agate has pale-blue banding. Its gentle energy promotes peace and harmony, and this crystal feels soothing and cooling. It encourages calm, clear communication.

Onyx is a black-and-white banded chalcedony often used as a protective stone. It has a slightly stern energy, which can help to clarify your boundaries with other people. It is useful if people have been taking advantage of your good nature.

Fire agate is a dynamic crystal with a deep-red colour that flashes with red, orange, gold and green. This warming agate promotes passion and supports sexual vitality. It may awaken strong rising Kundalini energy.

Dendritic agates have plant-like patterning that can aid connection with the natural world. Moss agate is a translucent chalcedony with green moss-like growths within the crystal. Tree agate is a white quartz with green branching patterns.

Suggestion for Use

Use a banded agate as an ally to work through a complex issue in your life. As you gaze at the centre of the agate in a quiet, contemplative way, focus on the current state of the issue. Move your gaze to the first layer of banding and let your mind shift deeper into the issue. Notice what lies beneath the surface appearance. Once you have recognized this aspect, take your attention to the next layer of banding and ask if there is another level to the issue. Keep moving through the agate's bands as you explore and gain a deeper understanding. Your insights may guide you toward a resolution.

Buyer Beware

Agates are frequently dyed garish colours. Bright pinks, purples, blues and greens are often seen in gift shops.

▷ Amazonite

Keyword: Integrity
Affirmation: I speak and act with integrity
Chakras: Throat, heart, solar plexus
Chemical formula: $KAlSi_3O_8$
Hardness: 6–6.5

Raw amazonite

Tumbled amazonite

DID YOU KNOW?

This crystal takes its name from the Amazon river. The South American tribal people who lived alongside the Rio Negro owned pieces of the stone and wore them as a talisman against snake-bites. They told the 19th-century Prussian explorer and naturalist Alexander von Humboldt that their Amazon stones came from "a land of women without men, where the women live alone". This links the crystal to the Amazons, the fabled tribe of fierce warrior women. The Amazon river itself has not yielded any deposits of amazonite.

Amazonite is a feldspar ranging from an intense green to more subtle shades, often showing white flecking or veining. Better-quality amazonite has fewer white inclusions and a pearly lustre.

Amazonite has been in use since ancient times. As well as its use in the Americas, it has been found as beads, carving and jewellery in Ancient Egyptian tombs.

This crystal encourages you to align with the truth of your heart. Although it may be easier to go along with the majority, exercising personal integrity is important, even when that risks becoming unpopular. Developing a conscious habit of speaking and acting from the heart is strengthening and improves personal boundaries and self-respect. Amazonite is particularly helpful in encouraging women to speak up for themselves in situations where they are outnumbered by men.

People recognize the energy of integrity and know that someone with personal integrity can be trusted. More importantly, if you develop the quality of integrity you know you can trust yourself.

Amazonite has been dubbed the "hope stone" because it engages an optimistic sense of what is possible.

Suggestion for Use

This visualization is for women who need the courage to make a stand and speak their truth. Hold a piece of amazonite. Imagine yourself as an Amazonian warrior woman. You carry a spear of truth and a shield of protection made from amazonite. See yourself looking confident and strong. Know that when you hold amazonite you can invoke your powerful warrior self.

▶ Amber

Keyword: Warmth
Affirmation: I bask in the warmth of the Sun's rays
Chakras: Solar plexus, sacral
Chemical formula: Organic composition varies;
typically $C_{10}H_{16}O$
Hardness: 2–2.5

Polished amber

DID YOU KNOW?

Amber is fossilized tree resin that formed
at least four million years ago. Some pieces
contain insects that were trapped in the
sticky tree sap. The idea that one of these
ancient insects may have fed upon the
blood of dinosaurs inspired the film
Jurassic Park.

Amber is not a crystal, as it is organic in origin and lacks a crystalline structure, but it is much enjoyed by crystal-lovers. It is light in weight and feels warm – rather like plastic – to the touch. Most amber is the golden orange-yellow associated with the colour amber, but rare blue amber is also found.

Historically amber was used in incense, as it burns with a sweetly aromatic smell. Nowadays it is too expensive to burn, but amber's younger cousin copal (a mere one to two million years old) is a common ingredient in incense.

Amber has a warming quality, encapsulating the energy of ancient sunlight. It is soothing and may give comfort if held to a sore throat. Amber is most welcome in the depths of winter when the Sun's warmth is a memory. It is strengthening for those who are convalescing after illness.

Suggestion for Use

When the weather has been gloomy, hold a piece of amber. Close your eyes and imagine the warm glow of golden sunlight bathing your body. Visualize breathing in the sunshine and see the golden energy transported to every cell in your body.

Handle with Care

Amber is soft and scratches easily, so it is best to save amber jewellery for occasional wear. It is heat-sensitive and will melt if held over a flame. Amber may turn cloudy if left soaking in water.

Buyer's Note

A lot of amber is reconstituted; it has been melted down and then re-formed. This gives more uniformity for jewellery.

Buyer Beware

Fake amber is coloured resin. It is sometimes used to make cheap novelties that appeal to children, such as keyrings containing insects. There are ways to test if you have real amber or fake. Try rubbing the amber for a minute on soft fabric to build up a charge and then holding it over fine hair or pet fur. Real amber will hold an electrostatic charge and attract hair.

▶ Amethyst

Keyword: Purification
Affirmation: I purify my energies
Chakras: Crown, brow
Chemical formula: SiO_2
Hardness: 7

Amethyst cluster

Natural amethyst point

DID YOU KNOW?

Amethyst gets its name from the Greek *amethyein*, meaning "not drunken", as the Ancient Greeks and Romans believed that amethyst could prevent intoxication. The wealthy and powerful would drink their wine from goblets carved of amethyst, keeping clear heads while their guests became drunk.

Roman mythology tells that the wine-loving god Bacchus was angry and vowed he would avenge himself upon the first mortal he saw. A pure and lovely maiden called Amethyst was on her way to worship at Diana's shrine when Bacchus's beasts leapt upon her. She cried out for Diana's protection and the goddess turned her into a pure white stone. When Bacchus saw what he had done he was ashamed. He poured a libation of wine over her, giving the crystal its beautiful purple hue.

Amethyst is a member of the quartz family and is one of the first crystals to appear in most collections. Its colour ranges from pale lavender to rich purple and is caused by traces of iron. Its calming energy can enhance meditation and support a peaceful night's sleep. It is traditionally linked to sobriety and is still recommended for those who wish to break addictions.

This crystal has long been associated with spirituality and was worn by bishops in the Middle Ages. It helps you to access spiritual guidance and wisdom. Amethyst clears the crown and brow chakras and may ease headaches.

An amethyst geode placed in a room can lift the energy for everyone who gathers there and may help promote harmony in a group. It is ideally placed in a healing or meditation room.

Amethyst is aligned with the violet flame of St Germain (see page 109), an Ascended Master who gifted this purifying fire to humanity.

Suggestion for Use

To relieve a headache, massage your brow gently with a smooth piece of amethyst. Alternatively, hold a palm-sized cluster of amethyst about 2.5cm (1in) from your head. Stroke it around your head in downward sweeps as if you are brushing your hair.

Handle with Care

Amethyst may fade if left in strong sunlight, so position it out of direct light.

Buyer's Note

Ametrine is a mixture of amethyst and citrine (see page 202), combining the properties of both crystals.

▶ Apophyllite

Keyword: Illumination
Affirmation: I illuminate my consciousness with light
Chakras: Stellar gateway, soul star, crown, brow
Chemical formula: $(K,Na)Ca_4Si_8O_{20}(F,OH) \cdot 8H_2O$
Hardness: 4.5–5

Double-terminated apophyllite crystal

Apophyllite pyramid

DID YOU KNOW?

The name "apophyllite" comes from Greek *apo*, meaning "away from", and *phyllon*, meaning "leaf". The name refers to the fragility of this crystal and its tendency to flake apart if heated.

Clear apophyllite forms natural pyramid-shaped crystals with brightly mirrored surfaces that reflect the light within, so that these crystals appear full of light. This is one of the highest-vibrational crystals and an ideal companion for healers. It is sometimes called the "Reiki stone" for this reason. Green apophyllite is a rarer variety and is aligned with the natural world. The best-quality apophyllite comes from Poona, India.

Apophyllite helps to clear the mind, making it an excellent ally for those who wish to meditate. Using apophyllite makes it easier to quieten the mind and maintain a meditative state without distraction.

The flat-based pyramidal crystals are popular for crystal grids as they direct energy straight upward. They may be used to grid a room, creating a sacred space for healing or meditation.

Suggestion for Use

Use apophyllite as a grid to create a sacred, high-vibrational space around you for a seated meditation. Sit facing whichever cardinal direction feels most natural for you. Place one apophyllite crystal at arm's length in front of you, one crystal behind you and one to each side of you, marking north, south, east and west. If you have a fifth apophyllite you can hold it while you meditate or balance it on the crown of your head.

Ensure you have a grounding stone close by for use afterwards if you feel spacey.

Handle with Care

Apophyllite has a high water content and is quite fragile, so do not expose it to sources of heat and handle it gently.

▷ Aquamarine

Keyword: Refreshing
Affirmation: I cleanse and refresh my energy
Chakras: Throat, sacral
Chemical formula: $Be_3Al_2Si_6O_{18}$
Hardness: 7.5–8

Natural aquamarine crystal

Tumbled aquamarine

DID YOU KNOW?

Aquamarine's name comes from the Latin *aqua marina*, which translates as "sea water". As the name suggests, it has a long-standing connection with the ocean. Aquamarine was thought to be the treasure of mermaids. The Romans associated it with their god of the sea, Neptune. Sailors carried aquamarine as a talisman to protect them against drowning.

Aquamarine is a blue to blue-green member of the beryl family, translucent to opaque depending on quality. It can be found as hexagonal crystals and in tumbled form. It is a popular choice for gemstone jewellery.

This crystal has a cooling, cleansing and refreshing energy. Aquamarine can be used alongside a detox regime, helping to flush the system of stagnant energies. It is particularly supportive of the urinary system.

Use aquamarine to release blockages in the throat chakra, enhancing clear communication and expression. It has a gentle feminine energy and its cooling nature may be particularly welcome for women who have hot flushes and night sweats during perimenopause and menopause.

Suggestions for Use

If you feel weary you can refresh your energy by visualizing that you are standing under a waterfall of sparkling aquamarine water. Let the cool, clear waters flow right through you, carrying away any tired or stagnant energy. You step out of the waterfall feeling cleansed, refreshed and wide awake.

To support a detox regime make an aquamarine gem water. Place a clean aquamarine crystal in a water jug and allow it to soak for a couple of hours, before drinking a glass of gem water spaced regularly throughout the day. The recommendation for good hydration is six to eight glasses of water daily, which is about 1.2 litres (2 pints). The water jug can be topped up after each glassful.

Buyer's Note

Deeper-coloured aquamarine gemstones have often been heat-treated to bring out the colour, as a stronger blue is worth more than pale blue-green shades. For healing purposes, choose the colour of aquamarine you feel drawn to.

▶ Astrophyllite

Keyword: Breakthrough
Affirmation: I make the breakthroughs I need to transform my life
Chakras: All
Chemical formula: $K_2NaFe^{2+}_7Ti_2Si_8O_{26}(OH)_4F$
Hardness: 3–4

Tumbled astrophyllite

Raw astrophyllite

DID YOU KNOW?

Astrophyllite was discovered in 1844 and named in 1854. The name comes from the Greek *astron*, describing the star shape of the crystals, and *phyllon*, meaning "leaf", which refers to the delicate leaf-like cleavage of raw crystals.

Astrophyllite forms eye-catching golden-bronze to blue-black bladed crystals that radiate in a star-like way. When tumbled, it shows a lustrous play of light, often displayed against a deeper-black background. This is a complex crystal, bringing together many different elements.

A stone of inspired breakthrough, astrophyllite is an excellent ally if you have been feeling stuck. It encourages deep introspection, so that you can identify where you have been self-sabotaging and how you have created blockages in your life. It then encourages you to gather your resources and skills to make the changes needed to burst through those blocks.

As an agent for change, astrophyllite may shed light on your shadow side, where unconscious aspects of your identity are hidden. The darkened recesses of your persona can be where your greatest treasures are buried. Once they are illuminated, you can recognize which aspects are potential strengths – such as suppressed abilities or skills – and which are self-sabotaging behaviours in need of healing.

As the name suggests, there is a cosmic aspect to astrophyllite. It often appeals to those who feel they do not belong on Earth. Holding this crystal may be comforting for these people, like meeting an old friend. Astrophyllite may stimulate memories of other lives in other worlds.

The stimulating energy of astrophyllite can bring cosmic light through the whole chakra system, from the transpersonal chakras above the head, right down to the Earth star below the feet.

Suggestion for Use

If you feel stuck, focus your mind on the issue as you gaze upon a piece of astrophyllite. Ask to be shown where you have created blockages and how you are keeping them in place. Allow your mind to go into a dreamy, trance-like state and notice the images and insights you receive.

Handle with Care

Raw astrophyllite crystals can be fragile.

▷ Aventurine

Keyword: Beginnings
Affirmation: I welcome new beginnings into my life
Chakra: Heart
Chemical formula: SiO_2
Hardness: 7

Tumbled yellow aventurine

Tumbled green aventurine

Tumbled red aventurine

DID YOU KNOW?

The name "aventurine" comes from a Murano glass-making process called *a ventura*, which is Italian for "by chance". The process was discovered in the 18th century as a happy accident. A glass-maker is supposed to have let some copper filings fall into molten glass, producing the sparkling glass called *avventurina*. The glass product lent the stone its name because of its similar sparkle. *Avventurina* glass is still made and is sold as goldstone.

Tumbled blue aventurine

Aventurine is a microcrystalline quartz that is most familiar as green with little speckles of green fuchsite mica that glimmer in the light. The sparkling effect is called "aventurescence", although not all grades of aventurine sparkle. Other colours of aventurine are available, including yellow, red and blue.

Green aventurine has an uplifting spring-like energy that supports new growth, whether that is beginning a new job, starting a project or embarking on a new relationship. It speaks of fresh starts and encourages optimism.

This is a gentle heart-healing stone which is especially beneficial for people whose feelings are easily hurt. These sensitive souls often feel bruised by other people's words and actions, even when they were not intended to cause any upset. Holding green aventurine to the heart chakra can help to relieve emotional pain.

This crystal has a youthful energy that engages the inner child in all of us. The child part can help us see the world through eyes of wonder; it is eager to grow and learn new things. Aventurine is an antidote to cynicism and world-weariness, encouraging you to take advantage of the new opportunities that come your way and to engage with them with curiosity.

Suggestion for Use

Hold a piece of aventurine whenever you are about to embark on a novel phase of your life. Close your eyes and take a moment to feel the energy that this new venture stirs in you. Notice the frisson of excitement, and allow yourself to feel curious and optimistic about the possibilities that lie ahead.

▶ Black Tourmaline

Keyword: Protection
Affirmation: I am strongly protected
Chakras: Base, Earth star
Chemical formula: $NaFe_3(Al,Fe)_6[(OH,F)_4(BO_3)_2Si_6O_{18}]$
Hardness: 7–7.5

Dravite crystal showing trigonal termination

Natural black tourmaline (schorl)

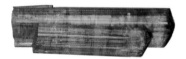

Natural indicolite crystal

Natural verdelite crystal cluster

DID YOU KNOW?

Black tourmaline is also known as "schorl". Its name comes from the mining area of Zschorlau in Saxony, Germany (previously called Schorl), where a large deposit of black tourmaline was found in a tin mine around 600 years ago.

Watermelon tourmaline slice

Black tourmaline is the most abundant and affordable crystal in the tourmaline group. This opaque black crystal forms naturally striated pillars topped with shallow three-sided terminations.

This is one of the premier crystals for grounding and protection. It has a stabilizing effect on the energy field and can guard against intrusive energies. Black tourmaline can shift stubborn energies and is a true crystal of transformation, assisting with the release of deep-seated fears and phobias.

If you feel you are under psychic attack, then carrying or wearing black tourmaline can help to shield you. Try not to focus on the situation, because thought-energy can add fuel to a psychic attack; instead, detach from the issue and any perpetrators as much as possible. Let the tourmaline do its work. Most perceived psychic attack is simply the energy of ill-will being felt by a sensitive person. Deliberate psychic attack is, fortunately, quite rare.

Suggestion for Use

If you are feeling fearful, use six pieces of black tourmaline to create a Seal of Solomon grid (see page 126) to sit or lie in. If the crystals have terminations, place them pointing outward to release any fear-based energy you are carrying. Once you are feeling less fearful you can turn the points inward to stabilize your energy field.

You can use black tourmaline in the same way to grid your bed, giving you a protected space to sleep in. Create a grid on the floor around the bed, with any terminations pointing outward so that they clear unhelpful energies as you sleep.

Buyer's Note

Tourmaline is a group of crystals displaying a wide range of colours. Many people enjoy collecting and working with them. Watermelon tourmaline is green with a pink core and is a tranquil heart-healing crystal. Verdelite is deep green and is also a good choice for the heart chakra. Indicolite is deep blue and excellent for use on the brow chakra. Dravite is brown, with an earthy grounding energy.

▶ Bloodstone

Keyword: Courage
Affirmation: I meet my challenges with a courageous heart
Chakras: Heart, solar plexus
Chemical formula: SiO_2
Hardness: 7

Tumbled bloodstone

DID YOU KNOW?

In medieval times it was believed that the blood of Christ fell upon bloodstone at his crucifixion, creating the red speckles and giving it magical properties of protection and healing. Its alternative name of "heliotrope" comes from Ancient Greece. *Helios* was the Greek name for the Sun and was their Sun god. Bloodstone may therefore be connected with both the Sun god and the Son of God.

Bloodstone is a microcrystalline member of the quartz family. It is an opaque dark green with red speckles or blotches. The red colouration of this stone comes from traces of iron.

This is a stone of courage and was used historically to strengthen the resolve of warriors. Bloodstone was also supposed to stop blood loss and heal wounds quickly. Fortunately, you are less likely to go into physical battle these days, but bloodstone may still bring you the courage and strength you need to fight battles in pursuit of justice, which may require a level of self-sacrifice.

Bloodstone is fortifying for physical health and is still used in healing to strengthen the blood. It may aid recovery from illness, can clear congested energies from the lower chakras and assist elimination, particularly supporting the liver and the bowel.

Suggestions for Use

If you have diarrhoea or constipation, place a cleansed piece of bloodstone in a jug of drinking water. Allow the water to become infused with its energy for a couple of hours and then drink a glass of water. You can top up the jug and drink a glass of water each hour until your symptoms have eased. If there is blood in your stool, your symptoms are severe or you are not responding to home treatment, seek medical advice.

Carry bloodstone if you have a difficult meeting, or a court appearance, where you will need to express yourself courageously. The energy of bloodstone can bolster your resolve to stand up for what you believe is right, especially where your bravery could result in a positive outcome for others as well as yourself.

▷ Calcite

Keyword: Playfulness
Affirmation: I lighten up, play and enjoy life
Chakras: All
Chemical formula: $CaCO_3$
Hardness: 3

Tumbled mangano calcite

Rhombohedral Iceland spar crystal

Rough orange calcite

DID YOU KNOW?

Iceland spar is clear optical calcite. It is believed the Vikings used Iceland spar's double refraction of light to navigate on their seafaring journeys. It was referred to as "sunstone" in medieval texts; the optical qualities of Iceland spar and its geographical source make it a more likely candidate than the crystal we now call sunstone (see page 284).

Rough blue calcite

Calcite comes in a wide range of colours and forms, each with subtly different qualities. The crystals share a "soapy" feel, which is most noticeable in raw pieces. Calcite cleaves easily into rhomboid shapes. Internal refraction of light, causing rainbows, is common in clear and translucent calcites. These stones are easy to work with, and gentler in action than most crystals. They promote a playful, light-hearted attitude. Use calcites if you need to have more fun in your life.

Iceland spar exhibits double refraction; if you hold a piece over text, you will see a double image. It can take you out of a narrow or fixed mindset so that you can see other possibilities.

Honey calcite comes in shades from palest yellow to deep honey. It is a translucent calcite with a soothing, yet uplifting and joyful energy.

Orange and yellow calcites are opaque and carry a cheering vibration. They are uplifting and encourage fun and playfulness.

Mangano calcite is light pink. It is one of the gentlest of all crystals. Calming and soothing in nature, it is rather like a crystalline calamine lotion.

Green calcite encourages light-heartedness and has a gentle healing energy.

Blue calcite has a calm, peaceful energy.

Red-brown calcite has an earthier energy and is gently grounding.

Suggestion for Use

Calcites harmonize well, so different types can be combined in healing. If you would like to have more fun in your life, try a chakra array using calcites. Start with clear calcites for the crown and brow. Use blue for the throat, green or mangano calcite for the heart, honey calcite for the solar plexus **and** orange calcite for the sacral, finishing with reddish-brown calcite for the base.

Handle with Care

Calcite is soft and scratches easily. This crystal may break along the lines of cleavage, if dropped.

▶ Carnelian

Keyword: Confidence
Affirmation: I can do it!
Chakra: Sacral
Chemical formula: SiO_2
Hardness: 7

Rough carnelian

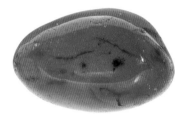

Tumbled carnelian

DID YOU KNOW?

Carnelian has long been revered as a powerful stone. Magical amulets carved from carnelian have been found in the tombs of Ancient Egypt. They were believed to protect the deceased on their journey into the afterlife. The orange glow of carnelian reflected the setting Sun in the west, which marked the gateway of Amenti, through which the soul travelled after death.

The name "carnelian" probably comes from the Latin *carnis*, meaning "flesh", although others believe it comes from *cornum*, referring to the fruit of the cornelian cherry, which is a type of dogwood.

This confidence-boosting crystal belongs to the quartz family and ranges in colour from juicy orange to more earthy orange-brown shades. Its colour comes from traces of iron oxide. Carnelian often shows beautiful concentric banding when polished.

It has an uplifting energy, which inspires a "can do" attitude. Carnelian motivates positive action and empowers you to take on challenges. Often the biggest and best opportunities in life take you out of your comfort zone. Carnelian acts like a cheerleader, encouraging you to go for it and do your best.

This crystal inspires creativity, particularly through artistic pursuits. It stimulates the desire to create things in general and supports the energy needed to see your creative projects through to completion.

Carnelian is a powerful feminine stone, which is aligned with goddess energies. The warming energies of carnelian encourage you to enjoy the sensual pleasures of your physical body. It can help you get in touch with your passionate, playful self and may boost your sex drive, as it supports the health of your sacral chakra. Carnelian can assist with healing issues related to sexuality, especially for women. It helps to alleviate feelings of shame or guilt.

Suggestion for Use

Carry or wear carnelian when you need a confidence boost. It is the ideal choice if you have a job interview, need to give a presentation or perform in public. Prepare in advance by holding the carnelian and visualizing yourself looking confident and happy as you answer the interview questions, deliver your presentation or perform at your best.

▷ Celestite

Keywords: Angelic realms
Affirmation: I am surrounded by angelic helpers
Chakras: Stellar gateway, soul star, crown, brow, throat
Chemical formula: $SrSO_4$
Hardness: 3–3.5

Celestite geode

Tumbled celestite

DID YOU KNOW?

Celestite's name comes from the Latin *caelestis*, which means "celestial" or "heavenly". Sometimes it is called celestine.

The world's largest-known geode was found in 1897 by workers digging a well in Ohio, USA. Initially the celestite it contained was mined for its strontium content, used to colour red fireworks. Fortunately, mining was halted and the geode was opened as a visitor attraction instead. The owners, the Heinemann Winery, say the popularity of their Crystal Cave saved their business during Prohibition.

Celestite is a pale-blue crystal associated with the angelic realms. It has a soothing and peaceful energy. The strontium content makes it feel heavy for its size, but it is fragile. Celestite is sometimes tumbled, which makes it a little more durable and easier to work with in healing. Larger celestite clusters are lovely when placed in a healing space or meditation room.

Support from the angelic realms is always available to everyone. Celestite helps you tune into angelic guidance by shifting your focus out of everyday awareness into a peaceful place of receptivity.

Like other sulphur-containing crystals, celestite can absorb heavy energies from the physical body. It can help to draw out and clear infection. You should seek medical attention if there is any concern about an infection.

Suggestion for Use

Lie down and place celestite at your crown chakra. Intend that you will meet your guardian angel. Relax and take a few deep breaths. Imagine you are floating gently upward into a heavenly blue sky. You reach a pure-white cloud where you rest. The cloud is shining with a luminous light and you become aware that you are in the presence of an angelic being. As you rest, you are bathed in light by the angel. You may hear loving words of guidance, have a vision or feel warmth and reassurance. When you are ready, thank your angel and gently float back down into your physical body. Wiggle your fingers and toes. Take a few moments to come fully round. Ensure you are grounded before you continue with your day.

Handle with Care

Celestite crystals crumble easily. Always handle gently and use incense or smudge for cleansing. When celestite is too fragile, angelite may be substituted. It has similar properties and is more durable. Place celestite out of direct sunlight as it can fade.

▶ Chrysocolla

Keywords: Gaia consciousness
Affirmation: I give thanks to Mother Earth
Chakras: Throat, higher heart, heart
Chemical formula: $Cu_2H_2(Si_2O_5)(OH)_4 \cdot H_2O$
Hardness: 2–4

Tumbled chrysocolla

Gem silica

DID YOU KNOW?

Chrysocolla's name comes from the Greek *chrysos*, meaning "gold", and *kolla*, meaning "glue". It is thought this was a reference to using the material for soldering gold.

Chrysocolla shows a swirling combination of vivid turquoise-blues and greens, often with brown inclusions. The colours come from copper, and chrysocolla is often found in combination with other copper-rich stones such as malachite and turquoise, when it may be sold as Eilat stone. Gem silica is the name used for chrysocolla that has formed with a layer of druzy clear quartz.

The appearance of chrysocolla is reminiscent of the Earth seen from space. It is one of the best crystals for tuning into Earth as a living organism. Chrysocolla has a feminine energy that is aligned with the goddess, particularly Gaia, who is the embodiment and intelligence of the Earth. In truth, Gaia's energy is around us all the time, but we often take her bounty and generosity for granted.

Over the last few decades human exploitation of the Earth has become so obviously damaging that it is clear to see that our collective behaviour is not sustainable. It is now a matter of urgency for humanity to shift from being users and abusers of the planet to becoming true caretakers.

By working with chrysocolla we become more aware of the size of our own environmental footprint. We are inspired to make more eco-friendly choices, and by living in a more conscious way we spread the environmental message to others.

Chrysocolla is a stone of true and harmonious communication from the heart. It is an ideal ally for teachers, lecturers, singers and writers who wish to share their message with integrity and sincerity.

Suggestion for Use

Hold chrysocolla. Relax and take a few deep breaths. Imagine the Earth as the goddess Gaia – a living, breathing consciousness. Ask her, "How can I help you?" Listen patiently for her answer. She may speak to you in words, pictures, emotions, or you may have an intuitive understanding. Whatever her answer, it should feel loving. Honour Gaia by following through on your guidance.

Handle with Care

Chrysocolla is soft and can scratch easily. It is quite porous and so may be affected by oils and lotions.

▶ Citrine

Keyword: Happiness
Affirmation: I do things that bring me happiness and joy
Chakras: Brow, solar plexus
Chemical formula: SiO_2
Hardness: 7

Natural citrine

Polished natural citrine point

DID YOU KNOW?

Citrine gets its name from the French *citron*, meaning "lemon".

Buyer beware: heat-treated amethyst cluster

Citrine is a translucent yellow member of the quartz family. It is usually pale yellow to yellow-gold, sometimes a pale yellow-brown. It is occasionally found as natural points.

Its energy is like bottled sunshine and it is probably the most antidepressant of all crystals. This cheery crystal can be especially helpful for those who struggle with seasonal affective disorder (SAD) in the winter months.

This is a crystal that supports optimism, encouraging you to dwell on the positive side of life. It is worth remembering that an optimist and a pessimist may be faced with exactly the same situation, but the optimist will see the potential for a positive outcome and will feel happier as a result. This is a more uplifting way to live. Optimists radiate happiness and joy to those around them.

Citrine helps you cast off feelings of lethargy or despondency. It encourages enjoyment of life and participation in fun activities, whether that is a social event, dancing, singing, playing a game or anything else that lifts your spirits and brings a smile to your face.

This crystal has been associated with abundance and wealth, probably because of its golden colour and positive energy.

Suggestions for Use

Lie down and place citrine on your solar plexus chakra. Close your eyes and imagine your solar plexus is shining with gold light like the Sun. Feel it expanding in size, warming up, energizing your whole body and filling you with happiness. Placed in the Feng Shui abundance area of your home, citrine can promote a healthy relationship with money. You may also wish to carry a small piece in your purse to symbolize abundance.

Buyer Beware

Most citrine on the market is heat-treated amethyst. It is more orange-yellow than natural citrine, sometimes orange-brown. Amethyst geodes and amethyst clusters are often heat-treated in this way. The more accurate trade name for this material is "burnt amethyst". You can still use burnt amethyst, but the energy is not the same as natural citrine's.

▶ Clear Quartz

Keyword: Clarity
Affirmation: My mind is crystal clear
Chakras: All
Chemical formula: SiO_2
Hardness: 7

Natural clear quartz point

Clear quartz cluster

Polished double-terminated clear quartz

DID YOU KNOW?

Clear quartz is often referred to by its older name of "rock crystal". It is cold to the touch and in ancient times it was thought crystal was permanently frozen water, hence its name, from the Ancient Greek *krystallos*, meaning "ice". The name "quartz" wasn't used until the 16th century.

Starbrary quartz

Clear quartz is abundant and found across the planet. It often forms natural points and clusters and may be water-clear or translucent. If you could only choose one crystal companion, then clear quartz might be the one to pick. It is a universal healer as it transmits pure-white light, which is made up of all the colour rays.

This stone amplifies the energy of any crystal it is used with. You can make the most of a small gemstone by holding it with clear quartz. Quartz often contains other minerals and will amplify the effect of the inclusions.

Quartz points can be used to direct energy. To help release stagnant energies, place the crystals pointing away from the body. Place them pointing toward the body to infuse the area with fresh energy.

Clear quartz can hold information within its crystalline matrix. It is the ideal choice of crystal for programming (imprinting the stone with a clear purpose). There are many specialist forms of clear quartz, each with its own metaphysical properties. Lemurian quartz and quartz "record keepers" are believed to be programmed with information from Lemuria and Atlantis. Starbrary quartz is thought to have been programmed by beings from other worlds. Many people believe these special forms of quartz have emerged at this time in our spiritual evolution to guide us through the transition into the New Age (see page 20).

Suggestion for Use
For a quick energy boost, sit or lie down holding two quartz points. Hold one in your left hand pointing up toward your wrist and one in your right hand pointing down toward your fingers. Relax and notice the flow of energy around your body as it is enhanced by the quartz points.

Buyer's Note
White quartz – usually called milky or snow quartz – has a gentler, more feminine and receptive energy.

▶ Danburite

Keywords: Spiritual guidance
Affirmation: I open my awareness to spiritual guidance
Chakras: Stellar gateway, soul star, crown, brow
Chemical formula: $CaB_2Si_2O_8$
Hardness: 7–7.5

Natural danburite crystal

DID YOU KNOW?

Danburite takes its name from Danbury, Connecticut, USA, where it was first found in 1839.

Danburite forms wedge-shaped crystals that sparkle with light. It is usually clear, but is sometimes subtly tinted with pink or gold. It has one of the highest vibrations of all crystals and resonates with the angelic realms. It helps to lift your focus from the cares and worries of the world to a place of tranquillity and harmony. Danburite aids peaceful meditation.

This crystal shines its radiant light into any situation, even one that appears dark. It elevates consciousness to a higher perspective and gives comfort that all is not lost, however hopeless things seem.

Danburite reminds you that guidance and support from Spirit are always available to you – you only need to ask. It facilitates a more conscious connection with Spirit and can assist those who wish to communicate with their Spirit Guides. Your Guides and angels are waiting patiently for you to invite their support, as they obey free will. True guidance will always feel supportive and gives you a feeling of being loved unconditionally.

Danburite's pure, high vibration makes it a comforting ally for those who are preparing to pass over. It sends a signal to their angelic helpers and Spirit Guides to assist the departing soul in crossing over to the Light.

Suggestion for Use
Meditate with danburite held to your brow chakra. Ask to connect with your Spirit Guide and take note of any inspirational thoughts, impressions and images that come through. You may receive clear messages; have a journal and pen to hand, so that you can write these down.

Handle with Care
Although danburite is relatively hard, its crystals are brittle and easily damaged, so handle them carefully.

▷ Diamond

Keyword: Eternity
Affirmation: I am an eternal spirit
Chakras: Crown, brow
Chemical formula: C
Hardness: 10

Faceted diamond

Raw diamond

DID YOU KNOW?

Diamond engagement rings are de rigueur, but it wasn't always this way. The De Beers group had a problem with falling prices and demand for their diamonds. In the 1940s they recruited an advertising agency, which created one of the most successful campaigns of all time with the slogan "A diamond is forever". Since then, diamonds have become the symbol of enduring love.

Although diamonds are usually colourless, coloured diamonds do exist and can be even more valuable. The most expensive gemstone to date was a pink diamond that sold in Hong Kong for £57.3 million in 2017.

Diamonds are made of pure carbon, which has been heated for millions of years under huge pressure. The carbon chemical formula is identical to graphite, which is very soft, only 1–2 on Mohs Scale. The heat and intense pressure that diamonds are subjected to causes the carbon atoms to form strong bonds. Diamond is the hardest naturally occurring substance on Earth, making it a popular choice for jewellery as well as indispensable for use in industry. The best-quality diamonds are cut for jewellery, but lesser-quality raw diamonds can be sourced for healing.

Diamonds get their name from the Greek *adamantos*, meaning "untameable". Historically it was believed that diamonds could not be damaged. This isn't true. Diamond's cleavage allows it to be cut, and diamonds can chip if they are hit hard enough.

Brilliant-cut diamonds are prized for the sparkling light they reflect. The bright lustre of a diamond is termed "adamantine". This scintillating play of light is a reminder of the spark of divine light that we all carry in our core. The brilliance of diamond can shine through heavy energies and help to dispel darkness from the aura.

Diamond is the ultimate symbol of endurance. Symbolically it tells us that we can withstand the pressures of life and come through the most trying of times stronger and wiser than ever.

Suggestion for Use
Wearing diamond jewellery keeps the energy of diamonds close to you.

Buyer Beware
"Blood diamonds" have been traded to fund wars, crime and oppressive regimes. Find out where the diamonds that you are buying were sourced. "Conflict-free" diamonds are available from ethical sellers. The Kimberley Process Certification Scheme monitors diamonds all the way from the mine, through cutting and setting to the point of sale.

▷ Emerald

Keyword: Alchemy
Affirmation: I seek the treasure within
Chakra: Heart
Chemical formula: $Be_3Al_2(Si_6O_{18})$
Hardness: 7.5–8

Natural emerald crystal

Tumbled emerald

DID YOU KNOW?

The Emerald Tablets of Thoth were believed to hold the secrets of alchemical transformation. The spiritual teaching "As above, so below" is a fragment of wisdom from this ancient source. The Emerald Tablets were said to have been given to Hermes Trismegistus. Hermes was the messenger god of the Ancient Greeks, often seen holding a caduceus staff. Alexander the Great is reputed to have used the knowledge of the Emerald Tablets to conquer the world.

He left the Tablets in Egypt, but from this point their trail runs cold.

In Christian mythology the first emerald was supposed to have fallen to Earth from the shining crown of the angel Lucifer as he was cast out of Heaven. Some believe that the Holy Grail was fashioned from this emerald.

Emerald is a green beryl. The colour comes from traces of chromium or vanadium. Gemstone-quality emeralds are a deep grassy green, translucent and prized for use in jewellery. Lesser-quality emeralds may be a paler green and opaque.

Emerald is the premier stone of the Green Ray, also called the Emerald Ray – this healing ray is a vivid green. Emerald is one of the most balanced crystals for heart healing. The Ancient Egyptians called emerald the "Stone of Lovers". Emeralds were dedicated to the goddess Isis. In Ancient Rome, emeralds were associated with the goddess Venus. Both are goddesses of love, beauty, relationships and fertility. It is still a gemstone associated with love and partnership.

Suggestion for Use

Hold an emerald to your heart chakra. Close your eyes and imagine a beautiful chalice carved of emerald appearing before you. It is glowing with a vivid green light. You are offered a drink from this sacred cup. You pause, aware that you will be changed by it. If you are ready, you take a drink. The emerald-green light enters you, opening your heart and circulating through your entire being. You sense an alchemical transformation beginning deep within your soul. When you have finished, the cup vanishes, leaving a green glow in the air that lingers for a while.

Buyer's Note

Emeralds may be oiled to enhance their appearance. This is an accepted practice and doesn't harm the emerald.

Buyer Beware

Synthetic emeralds are lab-grown and should be clearly labelled as such. Emeralds are often faked. Large cut "emeralds" from India are sometimes dyed quartz.

▶ Fluorite

Keyword: Focus
Affirmation: I am focused on my goals
Chakra: Brow
Chemical formula: CaF_2
Hardness: 4

Dark purple fluorite octahedron

Yellow fluorite cube

DID YOU KNOW?

Blue John is a rare British form of fluorite found in Derbyshire and prized for its beautiful banding. Fluorite glows under ultraviolet light. The phenomenon of fluorescence was named after fluorite.

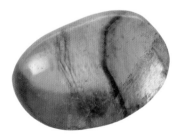

Tumbled rainbow fluorite

Fluorite is available in a range of colours, the most common being purple or green. Some fluorite displays banding showing several colours. It can form natural cubes and may cleave into octahedrons. These strong geometric shapes reveal the organized nature of fluorite. This is a highly practical crystal, which helps you stay focused, especially on tasks where the mind must be fully engaged.

If you are not a naturally organized person, then fluorite may help you put some much-needed order into your life. Work with fluorite to create logical systems that will help your life run more efficiently, whether that is organizing your home so that everything has its place, or planning your day so that you make the most of your time and do not fritter it away on distractions. Use fluorite on the brow chakra to help you arrange your thoughts.

Fluorite octahedrons help you keep your spiritual and Earthly energies in balance; the upward pyramid points to the heavens, the downward pyramid points to the Earth. In this way you can pursue your spiritual path while keeping your feet firmly on the ground and remaining practical.

Suggestions for Use
Keep a fluorite crystal on your desk and hold it while you plan your day.

If you are preparing to declutter, hold a piece of fluorite while you cast your eye over the area you wish to tackle. Fluorite can help you differentiate between what you really need to keep, what you truly derive pleasure from and those things that can be safely released. Once you have sorted through your possessions, fluorite can help you plan practical storage for the things you have decided to keep.

Handle with Care
Fluorite is a soft stone that is easily scratched and chipped, so it should be handled gently. It is light-sensitive and its colour can be bleached by sunlight, so store it out of direct light.

▷ Garnet

Keyword: Abundance
Affirmation: I am grateful for the abundance in my life
Chakras: Sacral, base
Chemical formula: Almandine garnet $Fe_3Al_2(SiO_4)_3$; pyrope $Mg_3Al_2(SiO_4)_3$
Hardness: 6.5–7.5

Faceted pyrope garnet

Natural almandine garnet crystal

DID YOU KNOW?

The Romans called garnet *carbunculus almandius*. "Carbuncle" was a term used to describe red gems in general; it means "glowing coal". According to the Jewish law book the Talmud, the source of light upon Noah's Ark was a large, glowing garnet.

There are several plausible theories about the origin of the name "garnet". It may have got its name from the Middle English *gernet*, which means "dark red". Another popular theory is that the name comes from "pomegranate", as it resembles the red jewel-like seeds of this fruit.

There are many varieties of garnet, but only a few are commonly available to buy in crystal shops. The deep-red garnet most used in crystal healing is almandine garnet, which forms naturally faceted crystals. Red pyrope garnets are more translucent and often cut for use in jewellery.

Red garnets have a warming and sustaining energy, which is especially welcome in the cold, dark days of midwinter. Carrying or wearing garnet can fortify you and help you gather your strength. Adequate rest and self-care are still important; no amount of crystal healing will work if your energy reserves are completely exhausted!

Garnet is strengthening for the base chakra and can help you feel more stable and grounded. It may assist you in feeling more present in your physical body. Garnets are useful for those who need help to bring their inspirations through from the realm of daydreams into physical reality.

This stone represents the cornucopia of the crystal kingdom, encouraging you to recognize that physical abundance already surrounds you. It helps you feel grateful for everything you have. Maintaining an "attitude of gratitude" is a positive mindset, which tends to attract yet more things to be grateful for.

Suggestions for Use

To feel more abundant, keep a garnet on top of a gratitude journal. Make a daily practice of holding the crystal while you list in your journal everything you are grateful for.

Bring your focus firmly into your physical body by lying down and placing three garnets in a downward-pointing triangle. Use two garnets on your lower belly, level with your sacral chakra, and the third at your base chakra. Relax and focus your attention on these lower chakras.

▷ Golden Topaz

Keyword: Mastery
Affirmation: I master my abilities and fulfil my true potential
Chakra: Solar plexus
Chemical formula: $Al_2SiO_4(F.OH)_2$
Hardness: 8

Natural golden topaz crystal

Faceted blue topaz

DID YOU KNOW?

Topaz may have got its name from the Sanskrit *tapaz*, meaning "fire" or "glow". Its association with the warmth of the Sun goes all the way back to the Ancient Egyptians, who believed that the Sun god Ra blessed topaz with its golden ray. It was thought that golden topaz emitted light and the 12th-century German abbess and mystic Hildegard of Bingen reputedly read her prayers by the light of a topaz.

The alternative name "imperial topaz" came from 19th-century Russia, where ownership of topaz mined in the Urals was restricted to the Tsar and his imperial family.

Golden topaz is valued as a gemstone for its beauty and durability. It is a translucent yellow-orange crystal that can form striated pillars.

This crystal encourages you to live up to your true potential and to master your skills and talents. Our abilities rarely emerge fully fledged into the world. We need to spend time nurturing, developing and honing them. True mastery cannot be bought or fast-tracked. It is said that to really master anything takes ten thousand hours. Perhaps the exact time needed will be shorter or longer for you, but you will certainly need dedication. Golden topaz supports you in sustaining the commitment you will require.

Golden topaz can also give you the confidence to allow your mastery to be seen and appreciated by others. Many of us have grown up being told not to boast or be big-headed, but other people will miss out if you don't let them see your talents and abilities. You can remain humble and still demonstrate mastery.

Suggestion for Use

Lie down and place golden topaz on your solar plexus chakra. Allow yourself to imagine how your skills and talents could develop and what you might achieve if you take the time to master them.

Buyer's Note

Several colours of topaz are available, including blue and clear. Blue topaz supports communication and expression. Clear topaz assists clarity of thought and perception.

Haematite

Keyword: Anchor
Affirmation: My energy is firmly anchored in the Earth
Chakras: Base, Earth star
Chemical formula: Fe_2O_3
Hardness: 5–6

Tumbled haematite

Natural kidney ore haematite

DID YOU KNOW?

In Greek mythology, haematite formed from the solidified drops of divine blood shed by the sky god Uranus when he was wounded by his son, Kronos. Haematite does contain a high proportion of iron and is still believed to be fortifying for the blood today. Historically it was used to staunch bleeding.

It is red when powdered, and there is evidence that haematite was used in prehistoric times by Stone Age humans as a pigment for cave paintings, as well as in their burial rites. The alternative modern spelling of "hematite" is commonly used.

Haematite gets its name from the Greek *aematitis lithos*, which translates as "blood stone". It shares this root word with haemoglobin, the red, iron-rich protein in red blood cells.

Tumbled haematite has a shiny silvery-grey finish. Raw haematite can form bubbly-looking chunks referred to as a "reniform habit". This is sometimes called "kidney ore". The surface of raw haematite is dull, unless it has been polished, and may show a powdery reddish patina, which is coloured by the iron oxidizing.

Haematite is one of the most deeply grounding of all crystals. Its iron content helps you connect energetically to the iron core at the centre of planet Earth. It is important for all healers to ground themselves thoroughly. When you ground deeply using haematite, you allow healing energy to flow through you and any excess energy safely dissipates into the Earth. In this way the planet benefits from healing too.

This crystal supports physical vitality and is still associated with strengthening the blood. It may be supportive for those with circulatory issues and any problem related to blood, such as anaemia.

Suggestion for Use
Sit or stand upright and place a chunk of haematite between your feet. Imagine a grounding cord of light dropping straight down and anchoring you into the core of the planet.

Handle with Care
Cleanse raw haematite using smudge, incense or sound, as it may rust if left damp.

▶ Howlite

Keyword: Restfulness
Affirmation: I am calm and well rested
Chakra: Brow
Chemical formula: $Ca_2B_5SiO_9(OH)_5$
Hardness: 3–3.5

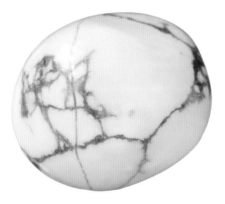

Tumbled howlite

DID YOU KNOW?

Howlite was named after the chemist Henry How, who discovered it in Canada in 1868.

Buyer beware: tumbled blue turquenite

Howlite is commonly seen as an opaque white stone with grey veining, looking rather like marble. It is readily available and affordable. It has a peaceful energy that is deeply relaxing and soporific. Howlite is good to carry if you are feeling stressed or anxious.

This gentle energy helps you release the cares of the world and disengage from life's dramas. It is a quietening stone, which can be a friend to sensitive introverts who feel bombarded by the noise and hectic activity of the modern world. It helps to create a peaceful oasis to restore their energies.

Howlite encourages an attitude of calm receptivity, which can make you a better listener. It is therefore an ideal companion for counsellors or therapists, assisting them in truly listening to their clients. It encourages a patient and tolerant manner. This quality may be useful for someone who wishes to work on their temper. It encourages taking time to "cool off" and calm down. In this way it helps the user come from a place of reason. Howlite is gentle enough to use with children who are having temper tantrums or acting out emotionally. Never leave babies or young children unsupervised with crystals as they could be a choking hazard.

Suggestion for Use

For a peaceful night's sleep, place howlite under your pillow or use it to grid the four corners of your bed.

Buyer Beware

Howlite is soft and porous, readily taking a dye. It is often dyed blue to imitate turquoise. This is sometimes sold under the trade name "turquenite". Although it is still white howlite underneath the dye, most healers prefer to use the natural stone.

▶ Jade

Keyword: Fortune
Affirmation: I count my blessings
Chakras: Heart, sacral
Chemical formula: Jadeite $NaAlSi_2O_6$; nephrite $Ca_2(Mg,Fe)_5Si_8O_{22}(OH)_2$
Hardness: Jadeite 6.5–7; nephrite 6

Tumbled jadeite

Nephrite jade palm stone

DID YOU KNOW?

Jade was valued by the Mayans and the Aztecs and used in their healing. It was named by Spanish conquistadors, who called the jadeite they found in the Americas *piedra de ijada*, which translates as "stone of the loin". It got that name because they saw the native people holding pieces of jade to their sides to relieve pain.

The Maoris in New Zealand also prize jade as a stone of good health and protection, and the Chinese have revered jade throughout recorded history, both for healing and protection. They still use jade to carve decorative objects, amulets and lucky charms.

There are two distinct minerals called jade, which can be confusing, but they do have similar properties. Nephrite is named after its traditional use of healing for the kidneys, *nephros* being Greek for "kidney". It is green, usually looks more opaque than jadeite and has a slightly soapy feel. Most Chinese jade is nephrite, but the more expensive imperial jade is jadeite. It was once so pricey that only the emperor and his family could afford it. Jadeite usually has a brighter, more translucent appearance.

Jade encourages you to feel fortunate and count your blessings. It is a stone of good luck and good fortune. In Feng Shui the money tree is called the "jade plant" because its rounded, succulent leaves look like pieces of jade.

Nephrite is still used to promote healthy kidney function. It supports elimination processes in general.

Suggestions for Use

Add a piece of jade to the pot of a money tree to symbolize an abundance of wealth and locate it in the south-east of your home, which is the wealth sector.

If you suspect you have a urinary infection, gently massage your back around the kidney area with a smooth piece of nephrite jade. Your kidneys are located on each side, roughly at elbow level. Drink plenty of fresh water to help flush your urinary system. If symptoms do not start to ease with home treatment, or if they worsen, seek medical attention.

Buyer Beware

Other green stones are easily mistaken for jade. "New jade" is used as a trade name for serpentine or bowenite.

▷ Jasper

Keyword: Strength
Affirmation: My energy is stable and strong
Chakra: Base
Chemical formula: SiO_2
Hardness: 7

Tumbled red jasper

Tumbled leopardskin jasper

Tumbled picture jasper

DID YOU KNOW?

Jasper has a long history of use as an amulet. It is thought the name comes from the Old French *jaspe*, which is an evolution of the Greek word *iaspi*, meaning "spotted" or "speckled".

Since ancient times red jasper has been used to fortify the blood. It was carried by warriors to promote strength and bravery. Some Native American tribes referred to red jasper as the "blood of Mother Earth".

Tumbled kambaba jasper

Jasper is a microcrystalline quartz that comes in a wide range of colours and varieties. In general jaspers have an earthy energy and help with grounding. In this way they stabilize the emotions and can be a real friend through challenging times.

Red jasper ranges from bright red to a brownish-red hue. Its colour comes from iron inclusions. Sometimes it looks as if it has broken into pieces and been glued back together with quartz – this form is called brecciated jasper. The quartz amplifies the qualities of the jasper. Red jasper has a strengthening effect for the body and mind that fosters a capable attitude. It has a stabilizing masculine energy, which can be useful for adolescent young men struggling to find their identity in the world as they move toward adulthood.

Picture jasper forms beautiful patterns like landscapes, which may be gazed upon in an open-eyed meditation. These landscapes can be explored in a shamanic journey.

Kambaba jasper is made up of stromatolites, fossilized blue-green algae that were some of the earliest life forms on Earth, existing three to four billion years ago.

The term for jaspers with circular markings is orbicular jasper. This applies to varieties such as ocean jasper, which can show a remarkable range of colours, kambaba jasper and leopardskin jasper, which has patterns like a spotted cat. Orbicular jaspers have a friendly energy that is comforting and nurturing.

Suggestion for Use

A jasper layout can fortify your strength. Lying down, make the shape of a rectangle around you to give you a sense of stability. Use four jaspers to mark the corners of the shape and imagine lines of light connecting them to make a protective and strong force-field around you. You can use the same stable shape to grid your bed, to give yourself a feeling of security while you sleep.

▶ Jet

Keyword: Honour
Affirmation: I honour my emotions
Chakras: Sacral, base
Chemical formula: C
Hardness: 2.5–4

Raw jet

Tumbled jet

DID YOU KNOW?

Queen Victoria popularized jet when she went into mourning for her beloved Prince Albert. After his death she always dressed in black and wore jewellery made of Whitby jet, which became the fashionable choice for widows.

Jet is not technically a crystal; it is the compressed and fossilized wood of ancient forebears of the monkey-puzzle tree. It looks rather like coal or anthracite, but is harder and will not leave a black residue on your fingers when you touch it. Some pieces still show the pattern of tree bark. Its depth of colour gave rise to the description "jet black". The finest-quality jet comes from Whitby in north-east England, and it used to be possible to pick up pieces from the beach. However, Whitby jet has become rare, and you would be lucky to find it these days. Most jet now comes from other sources, including Spain and Poland.

Jet is very light in weight. It has been used since prehistoric times and was probably worn as a talisman against evil. The Romans believed it had the power to deflect the evil eye. Its reputation for protection against dark forces continued, and it became a popular choice for rosaries and crucifixes.

Jet asks us to honour our emotions. As the saying goes, "Into every life some rain must fall." We cannot live and love without encountering bereavement at some stage, and mourning is natural and healthy. Jet helps us acknowledge our loss and truly feel our grief.

It can be useful for those empaths who readily pick up on the emotions of others. Jet can act like a filter, helping you to differentiate which feelings are your own and which are not yours.

Suggestion for Use
Hold jet to your solar plexus if you feel burdened by events in the news or situations affecting those you care about. Allow jet to provide a shield so that you can remain empathic without being overwhelmed.

Handle with Care
Jet is soft and easily scratched.

Buyer Beware
Anthracite is a form of hard coal that can resemble jet, but it is cheaper and will fade over time. The Victorians made black-glass mourning jewellery to imitate more expensive jet. Glass will feel colder to the touch and is heavier.

▶ Kunzite

Keyword: Grace
Affirmation: I am filled with grace
Chakras: Brow, heart
Chemical formula: $LiAlSi_2O_6$
Hardness: 6.5–7.5

Natural kunzite crystal

Tumbled hiddenite

DID YOU KNOW?

Kunzite is named after the great mineralogist George Frederick Kunz, who identified it as a newly discovered pink form of spodumene in 1902. Kunz worked for the jewellers Tiffany & Co. and assisted the financier J P Morgan in the creation of his remarkable collection of gemstones. More common grey deposits of spodumene are valuable sources of lithium for use in industry.

Kunzite is a form of spodumene that forms translucent pink crystals with striated sides. The crystals are dichroic, which means they display more depth of colour viewed from some angles. The colour comes from traces of manganese.

This crystal has a comforting energy that encourages a state of grace. It helps you move through life with a will to make the best of any circumstance, and to inspire others to look for the blessings in any given moment. In this way it brings about a feeling of contentment and divine grace.

Kunzite encourages compassion for others and gently reminds you that you cannot change other people, but you can always change your reaction to them.

The lithium content of kunzite has a sedative and calming effect on the mind, relieving worry and anxiety. Its striated form helps to shift blockages quickly.

Suggestion for Use
If you feel troubled, sit quietly and hold a piece of kunzite to your brow chakra with the striations pointing vertically upward, toward your crown. Breathe slowly and deeply. Allow a sense of grace to descend upon you, quietening your mind. You may wish to carry kunzite with you for the rest of the day and to sleep with it under your pillow.

Handle with Care
Kunzite will fade if left exposed to direct sunlight.

Buyer's Note
The pale-green variety of spodumene is called "hiddenite" and its green colour comes from chromium.

▷ Kyanite

Keyword: Detachment
Affirmation: I detach from those relationships that no longer serve me
Chakras: All
Chemical formula: Al_2SiO_5
Hardness: 4.5–5.5 lengthwise and 6–7 across

Natural black kyanite fan

Natural blue kyanite blade

DID YOU KNOW?

Kyanite's name comes from the Greek *cyanos*, meaning "blue". Kyanite has two different hardness ratings. It is harder to break across the bladed crystal than along its length. This unusual property gives it the alternative name of disthene, which means "two strengths".

The most common type of kyanite is blue, usually seen as single-bladed crystals. Better-quality pieces have a good depth of colour and some translucence when held to the light. Black kyanite forms fan-shaped crystals with multiple blades. Green kyanite is found occasionally with a stripe of blue running through it. Other colours exist, but are rarer.

Kyanite is the premier crystal for detaching relationship cords or ties. These form naturally between people in a relationship, mostly connecting from chakra to chakra. Cords are not a problem if they are healthy; on the contrary, they can create a feeling of closeness and rapport. For example, knowing what the other person is thinking, or what they are about to say, can be due to cords of light connecting at the brow and throat chakras.

Cords feel heavier if a relationship becomes dysfunctional. Unhealthy cords can be draining and may keep a relationship stuck in unhelpful patterns. Releasing cords allows you to step out of a relationship drama and assess the situation more clearly. Where a relationship is over, releasing the cords helps both parties to move on.

Suggestion for Use

Stand with a bladed piece of kyanite in your hand. Think of the person you need to release relationship cords with. Sweep the blade down the centre front of your body, making a couple of passes and imagining any cords being cut by the blade. Visualize making the same sweeps down the centre back of your body. Scan the rest of your body, noticing whether any other areas feel tight, which might indicate ties. Sweep the kyanite through your aura over those areas and notice if the sensation of tightness eases. When a relationship has ended, try not to dwell on the other person, because thought-energy can re-form cords.

Note: If you are fearful about detaching from the other person, perhaps because of an abusive relationship, seek help from a therapist who has been trained in relationship cord release.

▶ Labradorite

Keyword: Transformation
Affirmation: My life transforms as I follow my spiritual path
Chakra: Brow
Chemical formula: $NaAlSi_3O_8$ - $CaAl_2Si_2O_8$
Hardness: 6–6.5

Polished freeform labradorite

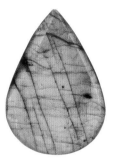

Labradorite teardrop

DID YOU KNOW?

An Inuit legend tells that in ancient times
a warrior struck labradorite with his spear.
Radiant colours were released. They flew
skyward and created the aurora borealis, or
Northern Lights.

Tumbled labradorite

Labradorite is named after the region of Labrador in Canada where it was discovered by missionaries in the 18th century. It is a type of feldspar and perhaps the most magical of all crystals, as it readily changes its appearance from dull grey to shining iridescent colours according to the way it catches the light. This play of light is called labradorescence. Colours displayed range from brilliant blues, to greens, pinks, golds and sometimes purples.

This crystal helps you to change your perspective and find the beauty hidden within even the most humdrum circumstances. Working with labradorite opens your awareness to the more subtle levels of reality overlying the physical world, which usually go unnoticed. This is a true shaman's stone, helping those who navigate between the worlds to shapeshift and journey safely.

Labradorite is a worthy companion for those undergoing the upheavals that often accompany spiritual awakening. It reassures you that true beauty awaits as you go through the process of transformation. Think of the metamorphosis that occurs when a caterpillar changes into a butterfly: if you interrupted the process midway it would look horrid, but given time and the right conditions, something lovely emerges. Labradorite encourages you to move forward in faith, even when things seem messy and the way ahead is uncertain.

Too often people say they want spiritual growth but then resist the changes that are necessary to make space for it. Sometimes you need to trust that there is a higher reason for your life being turned upside down, and that you will look back upon this time as a blessing in disguise.

Labradorite stimulates the imagination and supports creative problem-solving. Placing it beside the bed, or under your pillow, may bring insightful dreams.

Suggestion for Use

To protect yourself through times of change, visualize a magical hooded cloak made of labradorite, which surrounds and protects you. When you wish to pass quietly unseen, your cloak will be an unremarkable drab grey, but when you wish to draw attention to yourself and be noticed, it will radiate captivating coloured lights that shift and change as you move.

▶ Lapis Lazuli

Keyword: Wisdom
Affirmation: By seeking within, I find my innate wisdom
Chakra: Brow
Chemical formula: $(Na,Ca)_8(AlSiO_4)_6(S,SO_4,Cl)_{1-2}$
Hardness: 5–5.5

Tumbled lapis lazuli

Raw lapis lazuli

DID YOU KNOW?

Lapis lazuli has been mined for millennia and is the archetypal stone of Ancient Egypt. Its indigo-blue flecked with gold represented the cosmos, which was central to Ancient Egyptian beliefs. The stars were thought to influence the fates of humanity, a belief that has never gone away.

Lapis means "stone" and *lazuli* refers to the colour blue. Lapis lazuli was ground into powder to create ultramarine. This was an expensive colour and tended to be reserved for the most sacred uses, such as painting the cloak of the Virgin Mary. This deep-blue pigment is now produced synthetically.

Lapis lazuli heart

Lapis lazuli is a rock composed of several minerals. Deep-blue lazurite forms with variable amounts of pyrite, giving it the characteristic golden sparkles. It also contains sodalite and white calcite. Lower grades contain more calcite.

It opens a depth of understanding and inner knowledge. Lapis lazuli is a stone of the spiritual seeker, which teaches that true wisdom comes from within. This essential truth has been carried intact through the ages and across cultures. The words above the doorway of the Oracle at Delphi translated as "Know thyself". The Wiccan text *Charge of the Goddess* by Doreen Valiente states, "if that which thou seekest thou findest not within thee, thou wilt never find it without thee."

Lapis lazuli is your faithful companion on your inner journey. You cannot add one iota to your innate qualities – your quest is to discover them and learn to use them. Lapis helps you recognize your own true self and uncover your potential.

Working with this crystal may stimulate past-life recall of lifetimes in Ancient Egypt.

Suggestion for Use

Use lapis lazuli on the brow chakra in meditation. As you meditate it may open your third eye and bring personal insight and wisdom.

Buyer Beware

Some of the best-quality lapis lazuli is mined in Afghanistan. At the time of writing the country is still war-torn and the Taliban controls some of the lapis mines, profiting from the sales of the stone, and therefore it is labelled a "conflict mineral". Until peace has been restored, it would be more ethical to buy lesser-grade lapis lazuli from other countries. Sodalite has a similar energy to lapis, if you are unable to source lapis lazuli ethically.

▶ Larimar

Keyword: Serenity
Affirmation: I am calm and serene
Chakras: Brow, throat, heart
Chemical formula: $NaCa_2Si_3O_8(OH)$
Hardness: 5

Larimar heart

DID YOU KNOW?

Larimar is sometimes referred to as "Atlantis stone" because some believe that the fabled lost continent was located in the Caribbean, where larimar was found. It was discovered in 1974 in the Dominican Republic, which remains the sole source of this crystal. The Dominican man who found it combined his daughter's name, Larissa, with the Spanish word *mar*, meaning "sea". Larimar is also called the "Dolphin stone" because of its strong association with the ocean.

Tumbled larimar

Larimar is a rare blue form of pectolite. Although its dappled blue colour is reminiscent of clear tropical waters, it is born of volcanic action. It is relatively expensive and rare, but it has a supremely nurturing, soothing quality that makes it worth seeking out. Larimar is particularly helpful for women. Its tranquil energy helps new mothers relax into their mothering role. Its peaceful vibration can take the edge off hormonal mood swings, and its cooling action may help to reduce perimenopausal and menopausal night sweats and hot flushes.

Its energy is always calming and it provides an antidote to today's busy, fast-paced lifestyles. When you feel like you have no time for yourself holding larimar may instil a sense of spaciousness.

Those who have past-life memories of Atlantis may find larimar particularly soothing. Larimar's discovery at this point in human history makes it a true stone of the New Age. Its serene energy is a glimpse of what could be possible for humanity if we move beyond competition into a time of peace and cooperation.

Suggestions for Use

If you have been rushing around hold or wear larimar over your heart chakra to restore a sense of serenity and inner peace. Take a few deep breaths into your heart centre, creating a calm space for yourself in a busy day.

Run a warm bath and light a candle. Hold a piece of larimar to your heart and close your eyes. Visualize bathing in warm tropical seas. Imagine gentle waves lapping over your body, carrying away any stresses or worries.

▷ Lepidolite

Keyword: Peace
Affirmation: I replenish myself in peace and quiet
Chakras: Crown, brow, heart
Chemical formula: $K(Li,Al)_3(Al,Si_3)O_{10}(OH,F)_2$
Hardness: 2.5–3

Lepidolite "book"

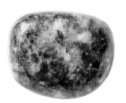

Tumbled lepidolite

DID YOU KNOW?

Lepidolite's name was originally "lilalite", referring to its lilac colour. It was renamed lepidolite from the Greek *lepidos*, which means "scale", referring to its layered, scaly structure. It is sometimes called the "grandmother stone" in acknowledgement of its comforting properties.

Raw lepidolite

Lepidolite is a lilac mica, which can form lepidolite "books" with a pearly lustre. These flat crystals are made of many individual layers of thin mica sheets, so that the edges look as if they are the pages of a book. Depending on the thickness of the book, it may be translucent when held to the light. Lepidolite is also available as microcrystalline tumblestones, which range from pale lilac to a deeper purple and usually display glinting flecks of mica.

If you seek relief from stress and anxiety, lepidolite may be an excellent choice as it is one of the most tranquil of all crystals. Its high lithium content helps to quieten mind-chatter and it has a soporific energy, making it the perfect ally for a peaceful night's sleep.

Lepidolite aids patience, quiet and stillness and so is very yin in character. Everyone needs a balance of yin and yang for good health on all levels, and for most people the modern world has become much too yang, with a treadmill of constant activity even during leisure hours. Allow lepidolite's restfulness to rebalance you, shifting you from behaving like a "human doing" back into a "human being". It is during times of peace and quiet that you truly replenish your energies and open yourself to higher inspiration and guidance.

Suggestion for Use
Place a lepidolite book under your pillow to support a good night's sleep.

Handle with Care
Lepidolite is soft. Do not soak lepidolite books in water as the layers of mica may start to separate.

▶ Malachite

Keyword: Detox
Affirmation: I clear and detoxify my energy
Chakras: Heart, solar plexus
Chemical formula: $Cu_2CO_3(OH)_2$
Hardness: 3.5–4

Tumbled malachite

Fibrous malachite

DID YOU KNOW?

Malachite is an important ore of copper. From around 4000 BCE malachite would be heated in a fire to produce copper. This is thought to be the earliest example of smelting metal from an ore.

Malachite with circular markings has been used as a protective talisman against the evil eye since the Middle Ages.

Malachite is a striking deep-green stone displaying attractive banding and circular patterns. The green colour comes from its high copper content.

This crystal has absorbent properties and draws out heavy energies from the body. It is an excellent detoxifier where there has been an illness or infection. Malachite often feels heavy or sticky when it has been used in healing and needs careful cleansing afterwards.

Malachite is a good choice for supporting the solar plexus chakra, particularly where there has been a digestive upset. It can alleviate resentfulness and envy from the heart chakra.

The eyes transmit subtle energy and their gaze can be felt. How many times have you looked round because you sensed someone was looking at you? Although we prefer to think of the evil eye as mere superstition, it remains part of our language. Someone may be described as "giving you the evils" if they fix you with a hard, unfriendly stare. Belief in the evil eye is still widespread in some parts of the world, particularly around the Mediterranean and the Middle East. Malachite may provide some protection from jealousy, which is often the underlying emotion behind hostility coming from others.

Suggestions for Use

Hold malachite over your solar plexus chakra if you feel like you are receiving hostile vibes from others. Imagine it forming a circular shield of protection over the chakra.

Use this crystal to heal your heart chakra if you are feeling resentful or jealous of someone.

Handle with Care

Malachite is soft and easily scratched. Keep malachite jewellery for occasional use. It is a porous stone that can be stained by oils. Do not cleanse polished malachite in salt, as this may dull its lustre. Do not place raw fibrous pieces in water, as fibres may flake off.

▷ Merlinite

Keyword: Magic
Affirmation: My life is magical
Chakras: Crown, brow
Chemical formula: $SiO_2 + MnO$
Hardness: 6–7

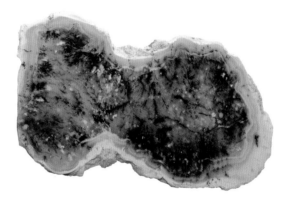

Merlinite slice

DID YOU KNOW?

Merlin is the most famous magician of the British Isles and a central figure within the Arthurian legends. Merlinite is a trade name for the combination of white chalcedony with black psilomelane, pointing to its magical properties.

Tumbled merlinite

Merlinite is a stone of magic and mystery. It is an ally for those who wish to work magically. The ability to weave magic is in all of us. Magic requires focused intent, and merlinite assists in focusing the mind.

When we work magic we must look at the bigger picture and ensure our motives are positive and are not driven by the ego. Avoid working magic that might interfere in the free will of others. Such workings are unethical and will backfire on you. The only real difference between "white magic" and "black magic" is the intention. As the maxim states, "Where intention goes energy flows."

Merlinite's black-and-white patterns remind us that we live in a world of duality where it is as easy to do harm as it is to do good. Each action has a reaction, and we must take responsibility for the choices we make. Merlin the magician was wise, but he was fallible. He was tricked and imprisoned in a tree by a beautiful enchantress. Merlinite urges us to look carefully at what is happening in our lives, seeing both the dark and the light.

The black psilomelane within merlinite encourages you to examine your shadow side and identify those traits that need bringing to the light for healing and transformation. The white chalcedony helps you to heal them. This inner work is the most important magic of all – the magic of self-transformation.

Suggestions for Use

To create magical change in your life, form a clear intention. Check it will not impinge on anyone else's free will and will not be detrimental to you or anyone else. Write it down, finishing with "May this or something better come to pass." By writing your intention you are literally "spelling" it out.

Light a candle and hold your merlinite as you state your intention out loud. Sit and visualize a positive outcome, feeling confident that your magical intention has been heard by the universe. Whenever you hold the merlinite from now on, you will be able to connect with your magical intention.

▶ Moldavite

Keyword: Awakening
Affirmation: As I awaken, my awareness and understanding evolve
Chakras: Crown, brow
Chemical formula: $SiO_2(Al_2O_3)$
Hardness: 5.5

Natural moldavite

Natural moldavite

DID YOU KNOW?

Moldavite is believed to be extraterrestrial in origin, having come from the cosmos in the form of an asteroid that hit the Earth around 15 million years ago, creating a strewn field over the area now known as the Czech Republic. Moldavite either gets its name from the Moldau river where it was first found or from the Bohemian town of Moldauthein.

Moldavite is a translucent bottle-green tektite. Technically moldavite is not a crystal, because the glassy material cooled too fast on impact for crystallization to occur. It typically shows surface patterns rather like tree bark in texture. Moldavite is increasingly rare and expensive, but it deserves its place in a collection as it has a unique energy that nothing else matches.

This high-vibrational tektite can open your awareness to wisdom from the universe. It helps you understand your role in the evolution of human consciousness, which is unfolding as we enter the New Age (see page 20). Moldavite may quicken spiritual awakening for those who are ready, although the intensity of this accelerated process is not always comfortable.

Sensitive individuals may find moldavite's energy is too strong for them. They may need to hold it for just a few minutes at a time while they get used to its energy.

Suggestion for Use

Lie down and place moldavite on your crown or brow chakra to support your spiritual awakening. Afterwards ensure you are fully back and present in your physical body. Have a grounding stone available to hold, if needed.

Buyer Beware

Fake moldavite made from glass has flooded the market. The fake material can be very similar in appearance to the real thing and is often priced just as expensively. It is best to buy your moldavite in person from a reputable seller. Hold it in the palm of your hand to test its energy. Most people feel the energy of genuine moldavite as anything from a mild tingling to a "moldavite flush", which makes the holder feel that heat is spreading rapidly through them. Fake moldavite will not give off any energy and will feel "dead".

Moonstone

Keyword: Receptivity
Affirmation: I am willing to receive
Chakra: Sacral
Chemical formula: $K(AlSi_3O_8)$
Hardness: 6–6.5

Tumbled moonstone

Raw moonstone

DID YOU KNOW?

According to Hindu mythology, moonstone was made from moonbeams. Ancient Romans also believed it was made of solidified moonlight. The Ancient Greeks called moonstone *selenitis*, after the Moon goddess Selene.

Moonstone is one of the most feminine of all crystals. It is a variety of feldspar, with a gentle pearly sheen, and comes in milky shades of cream, grey and beige. There are also peach and black varieties of moonstone.

Its energy is peaceful and receptive. Moonstone helps you to nurture yourself, relax and take time out. It encourages graceful receptivity and is useful for those who spend all their time doing things for others and don't allow others to help them in return. We all need to learn to receive as well as give. Moonstone is supportive for the sacral chakra and is traditionally used to heal feminine reproductive issues.

The receptive nature of this crystal can enhance your intuition. Insights come more readily when you are peaceful. You are more able to pay attention to the "small still voice within" when you are quietly relaxed.

Moonstone helps us to accept that all things pass – the good times and the bad. Like the Moon itself, our lives have their own rhythms and cycles. We cannot stop the flow of time. Moonstone can help us flow gracefully with the changing seasons of our lives. It is best charged in the light of a full moon.

Suggestion for Use

Lie down and place three moonstones over the sacral chakra in a downward-pointing triangle to honour the most receptive and sacred area of your body.

Buyer's Note

Rainbow moonstone is a white feldspar, which shimmers with a magical-looking electric blue in the right light. Its qualities are closer to those of labradorite.

▶ Morganite

Keyword: Compassion
Affirmation: I treat myself and others with kindness and compassion
Chakra: Heart
Chemical formula: $Be_3Al_2(Si_6O_{18})$
Hardness: 7.5–8

Natural morganite crystal on matrix

Tumbled morganite

DID YOU KNOW?

Morganite is a relatively recent find. It was named in honour of the great American financier J P Morgan, who was an avid collector of fine gemstones.

Morganite is a rare pink beryl. The colour is usually quite pale and, depending on quality, it may be transparent to translucent. It is a relatively expensive gemstone.

This is a gentle stone, which promotes a kind and compassionate outlook. It teaches the way of divine love, which sees beyond unpleasant surface behaviours coming from the ego to the cause of that behaviour, which almost always lies in suffering. Through the eyes of the divine, we are all children and we are all still learning. Morganite helps you release harsh judgements and clears the way for forgiveness. In forgiving someone, you are not making excuses for their poor behaviour, but you are releasing the anger and hurt that keep you stuck in the drama. In doing so, you make space for healing to enter.

Often we can be our own harshest critics, dwelling on our past mistakes and perceived faults. Morganite can help us find compassion for ourselves. In this gentle way we are encouraged to bring out our best qualities. Morganite is an ally for people who carry a nebulous sense of guilt, helping them to lift this uneasy feeling, which may stem from childhood events or even past lives.

This crystal can help dissolve emotional pain stored in the heart, literally easing heartache. By releasing past wounds and grievances the heart feels lighter and can be opened to love again.

Suggestion for Use

If someone has upset or annoyed you, lie down with morganite on your heart chakra. Allow yourself to imagine that person as a small child who is acting out their hurt or frustration. See that the adult's actions are coming from a similar place of upset, and understand that they are probably behaving badly because they are hurting. Send the child part of the person love and compassion. In doing so, you open the pathway for forgiveness and lighten the load in your own heart.

▷ Obsidian

Keyword: Shield
Affirmation: I am shielded and safe
Chakras: Sacral, base, Earth star
Chemical formula: 70–75 per cent SiO_2
Hardness: 6

Natural Apache-tear obsidian

Rough obsidian

DID YOU KNOW?

The form of obsidian known as "Apache tears" is found in Arizona and get its name from a legend dating from a sad chapter in American history. A large group of Apache warriors was camped on a mountain when they were attacked by the US cavalry. Many of their number were killed. Rather than be captured by the soldiers, the rest of the warriors rode their horses straight off the rock-face and fell to their deaths below. The womenfolk found their broken bodies and wept for their husbands, brothers and sons. As their tears fell to the ground they solidified, forming Apache tears.

Tumbled snowflake obsidian

Obsidian is volcanic glass, composed of around 70–75 per cent silica. The remaining content is variable; for example, mahogany obsidian gets its colouring from iron oxide. Technically it is not a crystal, as it cools too rapidly for crystallization to occur, although it is a popular choice in most crystal collections.

There are many varieties of natural obsidian. Black obsidian is one of the most common forms and is sometimes shaped into spheres or scrying mirrors. Snowflake obsidian has flake-like patterns of grey volcanic ash on a black background. Mahogany obsidian is a rich brown with black splotches. Rainbow obsidian shows a rainbow-hued sheen in the right lighting, which is often accentuated by skilful carving. Gold-sheen obsidian displays a golden iridescence when seen in the light. "Apache tears" are slightly translucent and look black, but are a smoky brown when held up to strong light. They usually have a tactile, slightly roughened outer surface.

All forms of natural obsidian are protective in nature. Obsidian readily forms a shield around you, so that unhelpful energies do not penetrate your aura.

Apache-tear obsidian is one of the best stones to comfort those in mourning. It helps with the grieving process, allowing tears to flow.

Rainbow obsidian and gold-sheen obsidian show that light can shine even in the darkest of times.

Suggestion for Use

If you feel worried or scared, hold a piece of obsidian. Imagine you are inside a perfect sphere made of the crystal, which completely surrounds and shields you. Any difficult energies simply slide off its polished outer surface and are grounded harmlessly by the Earth.

Buyer Beware

Blue obsidian is often seen in shops. Its trade name makes it sound natural, but it is simply clear-blue man-made glass.

▷ Opal

Keyword: Beauty
Affirmation: I walk in beauty
Chakras: All
Chemical formula: $SiO_2 \, n \, H_2O$
Hardness: 5.5–6.5

Raw precious opal

Fire opal in matrix

DID YOU KNOW?

Opal's name may come from the Sanskrit *upala*, meaning "precious stone". The Greeks called it *opallios* and the Romans *opalus*. Opal has an undeserved reputation as an unlucky stone. In a story by Sir Walter Scott the heroine wears an enchanted opal necklace and her fate is to end up as a small pile of ashes. This swayed public opinion against opals.

Older myths and legends portray opal as a stone blessed by contact with divinity. In an Aboriginal story, Creator travelled down to Earth on a rainbow and where his feet touched the ground, the rocks were transformed into opals shining with all the colours of the rainbow. Opals are the national gemstone of Australia.

Tumbled pink opal

Buyer beware: opalite

Opals are not true crystals as they do not have a crystalline structure; they are a mineraloid. They contain up to 10 per cent water and are composed of tiny spheres that refract the light.

The shifting colours, or "fire", of precious opals convey a sense of magical beauty. White precious opal has an angelic vibration. Black precious opal is aligned with magic. Fire opal may stimulate Kundalini energy. Common opal does not have colour-play. It is available in a range of pastel colours, is gentler than the precious varieties and is comforting and soothing. There is an opal to suit every chakra, from fire opals for the root and sacral chakras, through pink opal at the heart, to precious opal at the brow and crown.

Suggestion for Use
Gaze upon precious opal in an open-eyed meditation. Gently move it around to show the play of colours. The inner fire helps you appreciate the beauty and wonder inherent in being alive.

Handle with Care
The colour-play of precious opal may vanish if it loses water content, which can happen if it is heated. Store opals in a cool place out of direct sunlight. Never cleanse opals with salt.

Buyer's Note
In jewellery, opals are often mounted as "doublets" or "triplets". A slice of opal is laminated with other material to make the most of a thin sliver. When it is viewed from the side, you may see the layers. The jewellery contains real opal, just not as much as appears at first glance.

Buyer Beware
Opalite is a manufactured opalescent glass displaying a range of colours and is sometimes called opal moonstone. Common opal is also sometimes labelled opalite.

▶ Peridot

Keyword: Brightness
Affirmation: I attract bright new opportunities
Chakra: Heart
Chemical formula: $(Mg,Fe)_2SiO_4$
Hardness: 6.5–7

Faceted peridot

Tumbled peridot

DID YOU KNOW?

It is thought that peridot's name may come from the Middle English *perry*, meaning "bright", and *dot*, meaning "button". Others say the name derives from the Arabic *faridat*, meaning "gem". Peridot's name should be pronounced with a hard t at the end, although the rather posh-sounding "peridoh" has become the most common pronunciation.

It was mined for thousands of years on a mysterious volcanic island in the Red Sea that has had several names, including the Island of Serpents and the Island of the Dead. These forbidding names may have been designed to deter trespassers. The Greeks called the island Topazios and used the same name for the stone. The island's modern name is Zabargad Island.

Peridot is gem-quality olivine, with a brilliant lime-green colour that captures the light. Most tumbles of peridot are quite small. It is often set in jewellery.

This crystal is formed from volcanic processes, and on Hawaii it was believed to be the solidified tears of the volcano goddess Pele. It has been called the "evening emerald" because its colour seems to glow more brightly in the twilight.

Historically, peridot has been associated with protection from evil. It is still used as a stone of protection. It can be carried or worn to brighten the energy field so that heavier energies find no purchase.

Its bright appearance is in harmony with its optimistic qualities. It has a fresh, spring-like energy, which is particularly welcome after the dark days of winter. Holding or wearing peridot is a bit like taking a tonic and is enlivening for the spirits. This is a heart-healing stone, lifting heavy emotions and clearing the way for joy.

Suggestions for Use

If you have been feeling despondent or low, carry or wear peridot to lift your spirits and help you shift into a more optimistic mindset. Peridot helps you see that bright new possibilities exist.

Drinking a glass of peridot-infused gem water first thing in the morning has an enlivening effect on your energy.

▷ Petrified Wood

Keyword: Ancestors
Affirmation: I honour my ancestors
Chakras: Sacral, base, Earth star
Chemical formula: Usually SiO_2
Hardness: 7

Petrified wood slice

Tumbled petrified wood

DID YOU KNOW?

Petrified wood has turned to stone over the aeons. The tree's organic matter has been entirely replaced, usually with chalcedony, yet the stone will retain a sense of the original tree. Some pieces show growth rings and may even have stone bark. Patterns show up best in polished slices. Petrified forests have been discovered; one emerged on the coast of Wales in 2019. These are the remains of ancient forests that were flooded with mineral-rich waters for millions of years.

Holding a piece of petrified wood is a reminder that you are part of an immensely long chain of life on planet Earth. Each lifetime is an intrinsic part of the whole, and even though an individual life is relatively short, nothing is truly lost. The atoms that make your body will one day be transformed; they may form earth, plant or animal. Given the right burial conditions, your bones may even fossilize. While the materials that make your physical body are only on temporary loan, your spirit remains eternal.

Working with petrified wood may stimulate your memory. Recollections from early childhood can arise. Often these will be fond remembrances of relatives who have long since passed over and of the happy times you spent with them. If less pleasant memories surface trust that these are being shown because you are ready to process them and accept healing.

Petrified wood can also bring awareness of your ancestry. You have inherited a whole range of characteristics from those in your lineage, including your physical appearance and constitution. You may also have inherited intangible patterns, such as beliefs, behaviours and attitudes. Some of these may be positive while others may be a hindrance. Petrified wood can help you seek out the ancestral roots of issues that you carry and identify where healing is needed.

Suggestion for Use

Create an altar for your ancestors. Place petrified wood on the altar to acknowledge the long chain of your predecessors. Place photos of those who have gone before you on the altar, and a photograph of yourself in the centre. Light a candle. Thank your ancestors for your inheritance and contemplate whether you carry any ancestral patterns in need of healing. As you do ancestral healing for yourself, you can clear the energy back through the timeline. You may also avoid passing an unhelpful pattern on to your descendants.

▶ Pyrite

Keyword: Action
Affirmation: I take positive action
Chakras: Solar plexus, base, Earth star
Chemical formula: FeS_2
Hardness: 6–6.5

Pyrite cube

Pyrite cluster

DID YOU KNOW?

Pyrite is commonly known as "fool's gold". Its golden metallic shine has led many prospectors to believe they have struck it rich. Its name comes from the Greek *pyr*, which means "fire", because hitting two pieces together can create a spark.

Tumbled pyrite

Pyrite is iron sulphide. It may form natural cubes and dodecahedrons (a solid with 12 faces). Its iron content and heavy weight make it an excellent stone to use for dynamic grounding. Its sulphur content supports detoxification.

This stone's golden colour reflects the rays of the Sun and its warming nature. Like a beam of brilliant sunlight, it can clear cloudy energies from the aura. It is an excellent choice for energizing the solar plexus chakra as it galvanizes your willpower and can support you in taking positive action. This dynamic crystal can get you moving if you have been feeling dull or lethargic.

Pyrite has an assertive, masculine energy. It is one of the most yang of all crystals. Carry pyrite whenever you need to stand up for yourself. It boosts your confidence and helps you empower yourself. When you stand firmly in your own power, you may inspire and empower those around you.

Because of its golden colour, pyrite is often associated with wealth and abundance. It can be placed in the south-east, which is the Feng Shui wealth sector of your home.

Suggestion for Use

If you need to be assertive and want to feel invincible, visualize wearing a suit of shining golden pyrite armour. You can also imagine carrying a protective shield of pyrite to fend off harsh energies. Holding a piece of pyrite will remind you of your strong protection.

Handle with Care

Do not use pyrite in gem waters. It is best cleansed with incense, smudge or sound.

▶ Rhodocrosite

Keyword: Kindness
Affirmation: I treat myself with kindness
Chakra: Heart
Chemical formula: $MnCO_3$
Hardness: 3.5–4

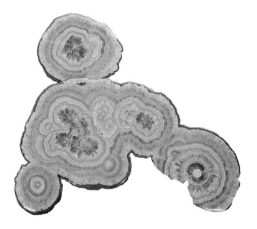

Rhodocrosite slice

DID YOU KNOW?

Rhodocrosite received its modern name in 1813 from the Greek words *rhodon*, meaning "rose", and *chroma*, meaning "colour". It is the national stone of Argentina and the state stone of Colorado. It was revered by the Incas, who called it "Inca Rose" and believed it was the solidified blood of their past kings and queens.

Rhodocrosite sphere

Rhodocrosite ranges from pale to deep pink and displays lacy patterns and banding. The pink comes from manganese. Translucent pink crystals also occur, but are rare.

This crystal promotes a kind and gentle outlook. It is easy to be critical, but we all make mistakes – it is part of being human. Rhodocrosite asks you to look for the good in yourself and others, rather than focusing on faults and flaws. It encourages you to be kind and, by doing so, fosters self-respect and tolerance.

Taking a more understanding viewpoint helps to heal old wounds, particularly those sustained in childhood when you may have felt unloved or rejected in some way. Rhodocrosite is one of the best crystals for healing emotional trauma and shame. With its compassionate and loving energy, it is the ideal choice for working with your inner child. Helping the child part of yourself to feel loved and safe can make a huge difference to your enjoyment of life.

Suggestion for Use

Find a photograph of yourself as a child. Look at the photo and hold a piece of rhodocrosite to your heart centre. Close your eyes and imagine the child part of you in front of you. Notice how it is standing or sitting and what it is wearing. Notice whether it seems happy or sad. Speak gently to your child self. It may be shy or wary, so be patient. See if your child will come to you for a hug. You may need to revisit and care for your child self over time. Do whatever is needed to ensure it feels safe and loved.

If this exercise brings up difficult memories, such as abuse, then you may prefer to work with an experienced therapist.

▷ Rhodonite

Keyword: Sharing
Affirmation: I can afford to be generous and share with others
Chakra: Heart
Chemical formula: $(Ca,Mn)_4(Si_5O_{15})$
Hardness: 5.5–6.5

Rhodonite slice

DID YOU KNOW?

Rhodonite gets its modern name from the Greek word *rhodon*, meaning "rose". Rhodonite was discovered in the 1790s in the Urals and was originally called *orletz*, which is Russian for "eagle stone". It was said that eagles often took pieces of rhodonite and placed them in their nests.

Tumbled rhodonite

Rhodonite is a striking opaque pink-and-black stone. Lesser-quality rhodonite may show muddier pink and greyish tones. Rare deep-pink translucent crystals sometimes occur. The pink colouration comes from manganese.

This crystal promotes a generous and sharing manner. It prompts you to ask how you are contributing to the good of the whole. If you feel you do not have enough to share, then work with rhodonite and you will be shown that there is always something you can give. A gift of time or energy is often worth more than one that costs money.

Recipients of your gifts may be friends, family, neighbours, a spiritual community or even people you will never meet. You don't always need to see the direct results of your contribution, or be thanked, to know it is worth giving. Sharing is not restricted to other people; your generosity may be extended to animals, nature or the planet.

Rhodonite is not a stone of the martyr, whose giving causes personal hardship that leads to resentment; rather it engages the spirit of the true benefactor, someone who knows they can afford to be generous. The heart-warming energy that comes from this kind of largesse engages the Law of Attraction, bringing plenty more for you to share.

Don't forget yourself. If you find it easy to give to others but are stingy toward yourself, rhodonite may be a good ally for you. When you are mean-spirited toward yourself it points to a deeper self-worth issue, which rhodonite can help you resolve.

Suggestion for Use

Sit with rhodonite and your journal. Make a list of the ways in which you share your blessings with others. Next, list ways that you treat yourself with generosity. If you don't have much to write, or there is an imbalance between your lists, think of other ways you could be generous. Remember that giving doesn't always cost money. Your time and energy are equally valuable. Keep adding possibilities until they reflect true generosity of spirit toward yourself and others.

Rose Quartz

Keyword: Love
Affirmation: I open myself to love
Chakra: Heart
Chemical formula: SiO_2
Hardness: 7

Rose quartz heart

Rough rose quartz

DID YOU KNOW?

In Greek myth, handsome Adonis, lover of the goddess Aphrodite, was mortally wounded by Ares, the jealous god of war. When Aphrodite heard the dying cries of Adonis she rushed to him and, in her haste, scratched herself on a rose briar. The blood of the lovers and Aphrodite's tears mingled together and fell upon white quartz, staining it pink. Zeus looked upon them with compassion and brought Adonis back to life for six months a year. Ever since, rose quartz has been associated with love, beauty and compassion.

Star rose quartz

Rose quartz comes in varying shades of pink, from pale to rich rosy hues. Generally the more translucent the rose quartz, the finer the quality. Star rose quartz contains tiny rutile inclusions that refract light into starry rays. Rose quartz rarely forms points and, when it does, they are usually tiny. You may see large rose quartz points on sale, but these will have been carved into shape.

Chunks of rose quartz in your home radiate a loving vibration. When placed in the south-west, they enhance the Feng Shui relationships sector, boosting love and romance. Rose quartz is often carved into heart shapes. These are ideally placed in the bedroom to symbolize love. If you have been alone for a while, rose quartz can open your heart to the possibility of new love. Working with this crystal can also help you recognize your true beauty.

This is the premier heart-healing crystal. Wearing a rose quartz necklace over your heart chakra can help you feel love and compassion, both for yourself and others. This stone is a great comforter in times of loss and heartache. Rose quartz makes a thoughtful gift for a friend or relative who is feeling lonely or has been bereaved. It has been known to take on so much suffering and grief for its owner that it has sometimes sacrificed itself, losing its colour and cracking. If a piece does break thank it for its service and bury it in the earth.

Suggestion for Use

Place several pieces of rose quartz in the bathtub when you run a bath, to feel more beautiful and put yourself in the mood for romance. You can swish a couple of drops of rose or geranium essential oil into the water and burn a candle to enhance the effect.

▶ Ruby

Keyword: Endurance
Affirmation: I have all the power and endurance I need
Chakras: Heart, base
Chemical formula: Al_2O_3
Hardness: 9

Tumbled ruby

DID YOU KNOW?

The name ruby comes from the Latin *ruber*, meaning "red". Burmese warriors would insert rubies into their flesh in the belief they would become fearless and invincible in battle.

In Sanskrit the ruby is *ratnaraj*, which translates as "stone of the king". Rubies have long been associated with royalty and often appear in crown jewels, although some of these "rubies" are actually spinels. The Black Prince's Ruby in the British Imperial State Crown is a huge uncut spinel. Spinels were not classified separately from rubies until 1783.

Ruby record keeper

Star ruby

Ruby is a form of corundum and is one of the hardest and most resilient gemstones. As a precious stone, ruby is often used in jewellery and the highest-quality gems are translucent red. In healing, more affordable opaque rubies are readily available and range from pink, through classic ruby-red, to a deep reddish-purple. Their colour comes from traces of chromium. Uncut ruby crystals often show their hexagonal growth pattern.

Raw rubies with triangular markings on their surface are called "record keeper" rubies and are believed to contain ancient wisdom. In healing, they may help you discover where you have given power away to authority figures.

Rubies sometimes contain fine rutile crystals, which refract the light into rays. These are called "star" rubies. They are often cut *en cabochon* to accentuate the star effect. These sought-after rubies have a more refined vibration, bringing the light of Spirit into matter.

This is a strengthening gemstone, helping to fortify physical energy and giving a feeling of robustness, resilience, courage and stamina. Ruby is an excellent choice when you need to stand up for your beliefs or call on your powers of endurance.

Because of their colour, rubies have long been associated with strengthening the blood. They may be used to bring warmth and passion into relationships. Placed at the base chakra, ruby is one of the most stimulating stones for Kundalini energy.

Suggestion for Use

Lie down with a ruby on your heart chakra. Visualize the ruby's energy flowing into your heart. As your heart beats, the ruby's energy is circulated all through your physical body in your blood, fortifying and empowering you.

Rutilated Quartz

Keyword: Inspiration
Affirmation: My thoughts and actions are inspired
Chakras: Crown, brow, solar plexus
Chemical formula: $SiO_2 + TiO_2$
Hardness: 7

Rutilated quartz point

Tumbled rutilated quartz

DID YOU KNOW?

Rutilated quartz is sometimes called angel
hair quartz or Venus hair quartz, because
the shining rutile resembles strands of divine
hair. Norse mythology says that when the
golden hair of the goddess Freya was cut,
her shorn hair was preserved in crystal.

Rutile is titanium dioxide. It can form radiating metallic crystals, but is most often available as an inclusion in quartz. Rutile strands suspended in clear or smoky quartz range from golden, through coppery-red, to silver in colour. These can be fine, ethereal-looking filaments or thicker strands with a bolder appearance. As with other inclusions, the quartz amplifies the properties of the rutile.

Rutilated quartz sharpens the mind and aids clear thinking. It has a quickening energy, which helps you get straight to the point. It is an ideal choice for writers, teachers and speakers, as it helps convey complex ideas with fluency and clarity.

The energy of rutilated quartz can shift stuck energy quickly. It is particularly useful if you feel bogged down or have been going around in ever-decreasing circles. It helps you find an inspired solution to an impasse, particularly where communication has been tangled or there have been misunderstandings.

Golden rutile assists in clearing the channel to receive divine guidance and inspiration. It helps you align your thinking with your Higher Self. It encourages positive, forward-looking thought processes.

Suggestion for Use

Meditate on an issue using rutilated quartz. You might be shown how and why things have broken down, got tangled or become stuck. Be open to receiving inspiration on how to move the situation forward. Have your journal to hand to note any messages of guidance.

▶ Sapphire

Keyword: Truth
Affirmation: I speak my truth
Chakras: Brow, throat
Chemical formula: Al_2O_3
Hardness: 9

Natural sapphire crystal

DID YOU KNOW?

The spheres on the Kabbalistic Tree of Life are called *sephiroth*, which translates as "sapphires". King Solomon's magical ring, which gave him power over demons, was reputed to be set with a sapphire. The British Imperial State Crown includes a sapphire taken from the ring of Edward the Confessor. In the 6th century a papal bull decreed that every cardinal should wear a sapphire on his blessing hand.

Probably the most famous sapphire of modern times is the one that Lady Diana Spencer received as an engagement ring from Prince Charles. Sapphire was her choice, and at the time it was scorned as a "commoner's ring" by a critical press, but she set a fashion for sapphire engagement rings.

Sapphire record keeper

Faceted sapphire

Sapphire gets its name from the Latin *saphirus* or the Greek *sappheiros*, both words meaning the colour blue. It has a long history of association with heavenly properties, probably due to its colour reflecting the blue of the sky.

Sapphire is a form of corundum. We tend to think of sapphires as blue, but a range of corundum colours are classed as sapphires. The main exception is red corundum, which is ruby. Blue sapphire gets its colour from traces of iron and titanium. It is an enduring stone and gem-quality pieces are often cut for use in jewellery. Lesser-quality opaque sapphires can be used in healing.

Sapphires are sometimes found with triangular markings. These are called "record keepers" and many believe they contain encoded information. "Star" sapphires refract light in rays. This effect is caused by fine inclusions of rutile. These are much sought-after and have a higher vibration, bringing the light of the divine into human consciousness. Star sapphires are usually cut *en cabochon* to enhance the effect.

Blue sapphire is the premier stone of the Blue Ray, which has a purifying energy. It inspires hope and trust. It has an energy that promotes a calm certainty, helping users to find their voice and speak up for themselves. It encourages speaking the truth, even when a viewpoint or belief is not widely accepted or agreed with. Sapphire can help the brow and throat chakras work in unison so that higher perceptions may be communicated with clarity.

Suggestion for Use

Use blue sapphire if you need to find your voice. Wear a sapphire ring on your writing hand to align your energy with the divine and assert your intention to communicate the truth.

▶ Selenite

Keyword: Cleansing
Affirmation: I cleanse my energy
Chakras: Stellar gateway, soul star, crown
Chemical formula: $CaSO_4 \cdot 2H_2O$
Hardness: 2

Natural selenite crystal

Satin-spar tower

DID YOU KNOW?

Selenite's name comes from the Greek moon goddess Selene. The largest crystals on Earth were discovered in 2000 in the Cave of the Crystals in Chihuahua, Mexico. The huge selenite crystals were up to 12m (40ft) long and gave the cave a cool and icy appearance, but conditions were so hot and humid that special protective equipment had to be worn to enter. The owners allowed the cave to re-flood in 2015, as the pumps required for their mining operations were switched off.

Selenite is a form of gypsum. Selenite crystals range from water-clear to translucent wands with wedge-shaped terminations. The more commonly available form of gypsum called satin spar has a similar energy and is usually sold as selenite.

Selenite has a feminine energy, as its goddess-inspired name suggests. It is a high-vibrational stone, which is refreshing when swept through the aura. Its purifying action feels rather like a cool breeze blowing away the cobwebs.

Satin spar is often carved into towers that look like fairytale castles. These can uplift the energy of a meditation or healing space.

Suggestion for Use

Use a wand of selenite, or a stick of satin spar, to cleanse your aura. Sweep it downward through your aura, imagining it brushing away any sticky or heavy energies. Imagine continuing this sweeping action around your back. To finish, stroke the selenite all round the outside of your aura, visualizing it mending any small holes and sealing you in a protective white crystalline bubble.

Handle with Care

Selenite is soft and requires careful handling as it is water-sensitive. Charging in moonlight is ideal. Keep an eye on the weather forecast and don't let it get rained on. Bring it in before morning dew forms.

Satin-spar selenite may fall apart along its crystalline structure if it is soaked. Cleanse selenite in smudge or incense. If it gets physically dirty and you really must wash it, then expose it to water for the shortest possible time and dry it immediately to minimize the risk of damage.

▷ Seraphinite

Keyword: Wholeness
Affirmation: I love and accept my whole self
Chakra: Heart
Chemical formula: $Mg_5Al(AlSi_3O_{10})(OH)_8$
Hardness: 2–2.5

Seraphinite slice

Tumbled seraphinite

DID YOU KNOW?

Seraphinite's name comes from the Seraphim, the highest order of angels, believed to guard the throne of God.

Seraphinite is a form of clinichlore, sometimes sold as chlorite jade. It is deep green with feathery silver-green patterns that catch the light with a velvety lustre. These show best where the crystal has been polished.

Seraphinite is a stone that connects you with the natural world. It encourages you to benefit from the healing that comes from being outdoors in nature. It has a higher, more angelic vibration than most green stones. It feels like the crystalline embodiment of the popular teaching from the Talmud, "Every blade of grass has an angel that bends over it and whispers, 'Grow! Grow!'" Like those blades of grass, each of us has a guardian angel who will never desert us. This heavenly being is not sitting remotely on a distant cloud strumming a harp, but is close beside us; we just need to tune into its gentle whispers of encouragement.

Seraphinite is one of the premier crystals for healing, holding a template for perfect growth. To be healed is to be whole. The roots of the words "whole", "healing" and "holy" are all the same. Nothing can be left out – there are no exceptions to be made. True healing is a radical process of self-acceptance and honouring your whole self.

Suggestion for Use
Hold a piece of seraphinite to your heart chakra and imagine that the feathery wings of your guardian angel are wrapping gently around you, infusing your whole being with light and healing energy. Imagine the voice of your angel whispering words of gentle encouragement, helping you to love and accept your whole self.

Handle with Care
Seraphinite is soft, so handle it gently.

▶ Serpentine

Keyword: Fearlessness
Affirmation: I overcome my fears
Chakras: Heart, solar plexus
Chemical formula: $Mg_6(OH)_8Si_4O_{10}$
Hardness: 3–4

Serpentine egg

Rough serpentine

DID YOU KNOW?

Serpentine has been used as an amulet for thousands of years. It was believed to offer effective protection against snake bites. It was given its name by the mineralogist Georgius Agricola in 1564, from the Latin *serpens*, meaning "snake". Some of the best-quality serpentine comes, rather appropriately, from the English area called The Lizard, in Cornwall.

Serpentine is a mottled opaque green stone whose patterning resembles snakeskin. It is easy to see where the ancient belief that this stone could protect against snakes came from.

This crystal helps to dispel fear, whether that is from real and present threats or more nebulous phobias, which can be just as debilitating. Serpentine may help you release old patterns of fear that you have carried with you from childhood, or even other lifetimes. Many phobias make little sense when taken in the context of this lifetime, but become completely understandable when seen from the vantage point of a past-life experience. You do not always need to remember the event that created the phobia; it can be enough to acknowledge that your fear probably has its foundation in the past, that there is no longer a threat and it can therefore be safely released.

Suggestion for Use

Hold a piece of serpentine as you contemplate a persistent fear or phobia. Breathe deeply and evenly and allow that fear to come up in your awareness. Notice where in your body you sense the fear energy, and hold the serpentine to that place. Keep breathing into that area of your body, with the intention that you are releasing the fear with every out-breath.

You may have to repeat this exercise several times, but you should notice the energy of fear getting weaker each time you do it. If you experience strong fear reactions, such as shaking or a panic attack, you may need help from a therapist who can help you work through your fear.

Handle with Care

Serpentine is a name used for a group of minerals, including a raw fibrous form called chrysotile, which is a source of asbestos. Avoid handling raw fibrous chrysotile, as it may release tiny fibres that can be damaging for your lungs, if inhaled.

▷ Smoky Quartz

Keyword: Release
Affirmation: I release that which no longer serves me
Chakras: Solar plexus, sacral, base, Earth star
Chemical formula: SiO_2
Hardness: 7

Smoky quartz point

Smoky quartz cluster

Tumbled smoky quartz

DID YOU KNOW?

Smoky quartz is the national stone of Scotland. It was first mined by the Celts in the Cairngorm Mountains in the Scottish Highlands around 300 BCE. They called the yellow-brown crystals "cairngorm" and used them for protection in kilt pins and brooches.

A smoky quartz sphere in the British Museum is thought to have belonged to John Dee, an occultist, seer and adviser to Queen Elizabeth I. He used it for scrying, calling it his "shew stone".

Natural smoky quartz obtains its colour from irradiation while it is in the Earth. It ranges from a pale-brown transparent crystal to deep brown, almost black. Smoky quartz is a gentle grounding crystal, which is helpful for those who find more strongly grounding stones, such as haematite, challenging to use. It has a purifying action, helping you release old energies that no longer serve you.

This crystal has a calming and quelling influence, which can be useful for stabilizing mood swings. It can be easier to work with than clear quartz if your emotions are volatile. It may help those who easily lose their temper to learn to control their anger and ground their frustrations harmlessly into the Earth.

Smoky quartz has a clearing, detoxifying action, which can support a dietary cleanse. Drinking smoky quartz gem water may help to release old stagnant energies from your system. Seek medical guidance if you intend to follow a prolonged cleansing regime.

Suggestion for Use

To purify your energy, lie in a Seal of Solomon (see page 126) created from six smoky quartz points. Relax and visualize the crystals drawing out heavy and unhelpful energies from your body. Afterwards have a warm bath and rest. Cleanse the crystals well when you have completed this exercise.

Buyer Beware

Much of the smoky quartz on sale came out of the ground as clear quartz and has been artificially irradiated to increase its value. It can be hard to tell the difference by sight, but artificially irradiated smoky quartz may still show white quartz crystal at the base. You can use artificially irradiated crystals, but may prefer smoky quartz made naturally by Mother Earth.

▷ Sodalite

Keyword: Discernment
Affirmation: I discern through appearances to the truth
Chakras: Brow, throat
Chemical formula: $Na_8(Al_6Si_6O_{24})Cl_2$
Hardness: 5.5–6

Tumbled sodalite

Rough sodalite

DID YOU KNOW?

Sodalite gets its name from the sodium
in its chemical formula. It is a relatively
recent discovery, first being identified
in the 19th century. Sodalite has been
dubbed "the poet's stone" because it aids
eloquent communication.

Sodalite is an indigo-blue crystal that usually shows some white calcite veining. It is helpful in gaining insights, and shows what lies beneath surface appearances. This stone is an excellent ally for those doing research, as it encourages digging deeply to discover the truth and filtering out distracting information and misleading data.

Sodalite encourages introspection and the ability to enquire within. In doing so, it helps you pierce layers of social conditioning and habitual behaviours to discern your true nature. Many people fear enquiring too deeply into their own nature in case they uncover something ugly about themselves. The truth is usually more beautiful than they dare to imagine.

Sodalite may help clarify your psychic perception and support you in trusting those flashes of insight that are easy to discount as "just my imagination". It takes a while to accept that reliable information can be received in this way. Maintaining a healthy level of scepticism is protective and helps you keep your feet planted firmly on the ground. Sodalite encourages you to practise the discrimination required to discern insights from wishful thinking and mind-chatter.

Those people who work with words – including poets, writers, teachers and public speakers – may enjoy the support of sodalite. It helps with communicating deeper truths and maintaining personal integrity, even when there is pressure to conform.

Suggestion for Use

Lie down and place sodalite on your brow chakra. Close your eyes and pay attention to images that arise in your mind's eye, or insights that emerge. When you have finished, make a note of them in your journal. Over time you will be able to discern whether these insights and images were reliable and helpful.

▶ Sugilite

Keyword: Shift
Affirmation: I shift out of old habitual patterns and step into the new
Chakras: Crown, brow
Chemical formula: $KNa_2Fe_3^{+2}(Li_3Si_{12})O_{30}$
Hardness: 6–6.5

Rough sugilite

Tumbled sugilite

DID YOU KNOW?

Sugilite is a relatively recent discovery named after Ken-ichi Sugi, the Japanese geologist who discovered it in 1944. It is sometimes sold under the trade names of "luvulite" and "Royal Lazel".

Sugilite is an opaque purple crystal that often contains black inclusions. It is relatively rare and expensive. Gem-quality sugilite is even rarer and is a translucent purple-magenta.

This is a true stone of the New Age, being unearthed in time to support humanity through this period of great transformation. It is a stone of the Violet Ray, helping to anchor high-vibrational spiritual energies onto the planet.

Sugilite assists in transcending the cycle of karma. We must become conscious of our habitual patterns of behaviour and shift beyond those that are unhealthy before the Age of Light can be born on Earth. It is time to let go of the seemingly endless cycles of falling out, schisms and grudges that humanity has indulged in throughout recorded history.

As you mature spiritually, you may consciously choose to detach from your old patterns of behaviour. Sugilite is your ally as you work through a personal clearing of karmic patterns. This is not a linear process, and some challenges may need to be revisited several times before a lesson is fully learned.

To shift out of the karmic cycle we must each do our own work and trust that by clearing our personal karmic debt, we will be lightening the load for all of humanity. Many believe there will come a "tipping point" when enough of humanity has shifted into a more enlightened way of being to usher in the New Age for all.

Suggestion for Use

Holding sugilite, sit quietly and review the repeating patterns and challenges in your life. Consider how you may have been keeping these patterns in place. Ask to be shown reparations that you could make and alternative ways you could respond to these situations in future.

Buyer Beware

Howlite is sometimes dyed purple to mimic sugilite.

▷ Sunstone

Keyword: Self-assurance
Affirmation: I allow my gifts and talents to be seen
Chakras: Solar plexus, sacral
Chemical formula: $(Ca,Na)((Al,Si)_2Si_2O_8)$
Hardness: 6–6.5

Tumbled sunstone

Rough sunstone

DID YOU KNOW?

Native Americans living in Oregon's Warner Valley were probably the first collectors of sunstone. A Native American legend tells that when a mighty warrior was wounded, his blood fell upon the stones. His spirit infused the stones through his blood, giving them their colour and power.

Sunstone is an orange feldspar, which shimmers with spangles of light reflected from fine platelets of haematite; crystals from Oregon contain flecks of copper. High-quality sunstone is often cut *en cabochon* to show off the play of light. Lesser-quality sunstone appears more orange-white and blotchy and is usually tumbled.

This crystal can give you the confidence to shine. It is not a shy energy, and it counsels those who would ordinarily hide their light under the proverbial bushel to allow themselves to be seen. Letting others see your talents and gifts is not egotism; it is about sharing your best qualities and abilities with the world. If you habitually let others take centre-stage and shrink from taking the lead in your own life, work with sunstone to boost your self-assurance.

Sunstone encourages taking natural pleasure in the body and letting go of learned inhibitions. It can assist in dissolving feelings of guilt and shame associated with sexuality. Whereas moonstone is a feldspar with a yin energy, especially healing for women's sexual health, sunstone has a yang energy and may be more supportive for male sexual health.

This stone is as warming as its name suggests. It is an excellent companion for those living in colder climes, especially through the winter months. It has an antidepressant quality and helps to motivate you into positive action – particularly helpful when you have been feeling sluggish or despondent.

Suggestion for Use

Holding a piece of sunstone, close your eyes and contemplate your gifts and talents. Ask yourself why you have been hiding them from the world. If you are scared of judgement or criticism, hold the sunstone to your solar plexus and allow it to dissolve the fear. Invite it to support you in finding the confidence to be seen. Resolve to carry or wear sunstone to step out of your comfort zone and allow yourself to shine.

▶ Tektite

Keyword: Cosmos
Affirmation: I open my awareness to cosmic energies
Chakras: Brow, Earth star
Chemical formula: 70–98 per cent SiO_2
Hardness: 5.5–6.5

Natural tektite

Natural Libyan desert glass

DID YOU KNOW?

Tektite's name comes from the Greek word *tektos*, which means "molten". Tektites have been revered as magical and sacred across the lands where they are found. In Sanskrit they were called *agni mani*, meaning "jewels of fire". The Tibetans called them the "Stone of Shambala".

Tektites are natural glass with a high silica content in variable quantities, according to type. They are usually black and form in the high temperatures generated when meteors enter Earth's atmosphere and collide with the ground. They may be partly made from extraterrestrial material, but are mostly terrestrial glass formed by these cosmic impacts. Tektites often have interesting droplet shapes and surface textures, which were caused by the speed of movement and rapid cooling of molten material when they formed.

Earth's atmosphere gives us protection against cosmic debris, most of which is space dust left in a trail by passing comets. These particles burn up harmlessly on entry, producing the beautiful phenomena of "shooting stars". Meteorites can get through Earth's natural defences. Fortunately for humanity, this is a rare occurrence. It is believed that the demise of the dinosaurs was caused by the impact of a large meteorite, which plunged Earth into an Ice Age. Tektites are found in strewn fields from meteoric impacts, some of which cover huge areas.

Tektites remind us that Earth exists as part of the cosmos and is subjected to cosmic forces. We are just a small part of the majesty that makes up the universe. Meditation with tektite may expand your awareness of the larger cosmos.

This crystal may help you if you feel stuck, as it was literally formed by an event that came "out of the blue". Tektite can bring a sudden "aha" moment of inspiration or realization.

Suggestion for Use

Go outside holding a piece of tektite on a clear starry night. Gaze up at the cosmos and contemplate Earth's part in the cosmic whole. If you can go to a place without too much light pollution, and time your outing with a meteor shower, you may be lucky enough to see shooting stars.

Buyer's Note

Moldavite and Libyan Desert Glass are translucent coloured tektites. These are much rarer and more expensive than the common black tektites.

▶ Tiger's Eye

Keyword: Stability
Affirmation: I stabilize my energy
Chakras: Solar plexus, base, Earth star
Chemical formula: SiO_2
Hardness: 7

Tumbled tiger's eye

Rough tiger's eye

DID YOU KNOW?

Tiger's eye has been used as a stone of protection and courage since ancient times. The Ancient Egyptians carved tiger's eye into magical amulets. It is thought that Roman soldiers carried this crystal for bravery when they went into battle.

Buyer beware: tumbled red tiger's eye

Tiger's eye is a member of the quartz family, with warm golden-brown banding that shimmers with a silky chatoyancy, caused by tightly packed fibrous inclusions that reflect the light. Tiger's eye is a true power stone, helping you stay firmly in command of your life. Think of the magnificent strength of the tiger with which it is associated.

It has a warming energy, which helps you regroup your physical energy. This can be particularly helpful at times of convalescence. Tiger's eye is a strengthening crystal, which helps you keep your energy grounded, even when the circumstances are challenging. It assists you in making subtle adjustments to maintain your stability as change occurs.

Tiger's eye combines the Gold Ray of healing with Earth's grounding energy, which makes it a valuable ally for those seeking to anchor the higher-vibrational energies coming onto the planet as the energies shift in preparation for the New Age. The influx of such energies from the cosmos can be destabilizing, especially for those who habitually feel ungrounded. If this phase of evolution and change feels overwhelming, tiger's eye may help you integrate the new frequencies.

Suggestion for Use
If you feel overwhelmed, or if your energy feels scattered, place a tiger's eye between your feet and hold another at your solar plexus chakra while sitting or standing. Focus on the crystal at your solar plexus. Build awareness of your strong centre, feeling your energy becoming more unified and stable.

Buyer's Note
Hawk's eye is a closely related blue-black crystal that also displays chatoyancy. Pietersite is a swirling mixture of tiger's eye and hawk's eye, which has been dubbed "storm stone" or "tempest stone" because it can be supportive through turbulent times of change.

Buyer Beware
Red tiger's eye is sometimes marketed as dragon's eye. The colour is usually produced by heating tiger's eye.

▷ Turquoise

Keyword: Centre
Affirmation: I centre my energy
Chakras: Throat, heart, solar plexus, sacral
Chemical formula: $CuAl_6(PO_4)_4(OH)_8 \cdot 4H_2O$
Hardness: 5–6

Tumbled turquoise

Raw turquoise

DID YOU KNOW?

The French named it *pierre turquoise*, meaning "Turkish stone", but it does not originate from Turkey; it simply passed through that country en route from the Middle East and Asia. Turquoise probably first arrived in Europe at the time of the Crusades.

It has been prized for thousands of years across many cultures, including the Ancient Egyptians, Aztecs, Persians and Chinese. Turquoise is the national stone of Iran, where it has been mined for millennia, and turquoise beads dating back to 5000 BCE have been found in Iraq.

Turquoise has been used with great artistry across cultures for jewellery and to inlay sacred and ceremonial items, including thrones, funeral masks and daggers. The Tibetans revered turquoise for its colour, seeing it as a reflection of the heavens. To this day turquoise is valued in Native American culture, especially among the Navajo, Apache and Pueblo tribes.

Turquoise gets its blue colour from its copper content, with greener shades containing traces of iron. The crystal has given its name to the colour turquoise.

This crystal supports you in staying peacefully centred, even when life is challenging. Centring with turquoise gives you the chance to restore and replenish your energies. Learning to support others without getting involved in their dramas is a part of this stone's teaching.

Turquoise may boost your creative spirit. What would you like to create? Making things is a basic human instinct. Ensure some of your creations are purely for your own enjoyment.

Suggestion for Use

If you feel you have over-extended your energy, it is time to replenish and restore. Place turquoise at your heart and solar plexus chakras. Put a hand on each stone and breathe deeply into your abdomen. Imagine you are recalling your energy. When you have finished, take time to rest.

Handle with Care

Turquoise is porous and can be stained if it is in contact with oils. Its colour can fade in strong sunlight.

Buyer Beware

White howlite is often dyed vivid blue and sold as turquoise. The trade name for this is "turquenite". Magnesite forms crystals with a similar nodular shape to turquoise; when dyed blue, it can make a convincing fake. Fake turquoise is nothing new – soapstone has been found coloured to mimic turquoise dating back as far as 3000 BCE. Buy turquoise from a reputable seller.

▶ Unakite

Keyword: Harmony
Affirmation: I seek harmony in my relationships
Chakra: Heart
Chemical formula: $KAlSi_3O_8$, $Ca_2(Al,Fe)_3(SiO_4)_3(OH)$ SiO_2
Hardness: 6–7

Unakite sphere

Tumbled unakite

DID YOU KNOW?

Unakite gets its name from the Unaka mountains in North Carolina and Tennessee, USA, where it was discovered in 1874.

Unakite is a granite-like rock, a composite mixture of pink orthoclase feldspar and moss-green epidote, which combine with quartz. Pink orthoclase is found as a component in granites and is sometimes used for the pillars and steps of grand buildings. In common with pink stones generally, it supports emotional wellbeing. Green epidote is a centring crystal that helps us to connect with nature. The presence of quartz amplifies the healing qualities of both stones.

This harmonious pink-and-green combination provides a perfectly balanced energy for healing the heart chakra. Unakite has a gentle action – like applying a comforting salve to ease heartache. It helps you let go of sad and painful memories and move on with life.

Unakite is a stone of healthy and harmonious relationships. It demonstrates that the whole really can be greater than the sum of its parts, showing the potential for mutual learning and growth that comes through relationships. It helps to support a tolerant attitude and can promote understanding of another person's point of view. It may support you in overcoming your differences and coming to fair agreements. This well-balanced composite can also help you integrate disparate aspects of your own being into a harmonious whole.

Suggestion for Use

To bring more balance and understanding into a relationship, lie down and place unakite at your heart chakra. As you relax, imagine seeing the situation from the other person's point of view. Open yourself to the possibility that both your viewpoints may be valid. Ask for inspiration on how you might come to an agreement that honours both of your perspectives.

Glossary

acupuncture: a system of healing from Traditional Chinese Medicine that treats the meridians by inserting fine needles to regulate energy flow

affirmation: a short statement used repeatedly to foster a positive mental attitude

amorphous: matter that is lacking a crystalline structure

amulet: a piece of jewellery or ornament that is believed to offer protection

ankh: Ancient Egyptian symbol of life, eternity and rebirth

Ascended Master: believed to be an evolved being who has lived human lifetimes and supports humanity's spiritual evolution

attune: the act of tuning into a crystal's energy to find out more about it

aura: the energy field that surrounds the physical body

awakening: the process of opening to spiritual consciousness

Ayurveda: an ancient system of healing that originated in India

beryl family: crystals containing the element beryllium, including aquamarine, emerald and morganite

centring: the process of gathering your energy and becoming present in the moment, a state described as "being centred"

chakra: a spinning energy centre that processes prana, or subtle energy

channel: to bring through healing energy, or to receive messages from discarnate beings

charging: filling a crystal with universal energy

chatoyancy: a lustre that shines rather like a cat's eye

chi: the Chinese term for subtle energy

Chinese five elements: the ancient Chinese theory that everything in creation is made of five elements: Wood, Fire, Earth, Metal and Water; five-element theory is the foundation of Traditional Chinese Medicine

clairvoyant: to be able to perceive psychic images or have extrasensory visual perception beyond physical sight

cleavage: the way in which a crystal breaks, or cleaves

cluster: crystals growing together as a group sharing a common base

crystal: matter formed of a regular and orderly arrangement of atoms and molecules in a three-dimensional shape, which repeats to create a lattice structure.

crystal grid: an arrangement of crystals that has been created with a focused intention

crystal layout: an arrangement of crystals often placed on or around the body

crystalline: pertaining to a crystal

crystallization: the process of a crystal forming

detox: the release of stagnant, congested or unhealthy energies from the body

dowsing: the use of a pendulum or other dowsing device to obtain guidance

druzy: a layer of tiny crystals that covers the surface of a larger crystal

earthing: making physical and energetic contact with the ground

Earth star: a transpersonal chakra located beneath the feet, which assists in making a grounded connection to the Earth's energy

Electromagnetic Field (EMF): the electrical energy that is emitted by and surrounds all electronic equipment

en cabochon: a gemstone that is cut and polished with a convex dome rather than faceted

endocrine glands: ductless glands in the body that secrete hormones

energy field: the non-physical energy, or aura, that surrounds a physical body

enlightenment: achieving self-realization and Oneness with all that is

esoteric: mystical or religious knowledge that is specialized and not generally known

essence: the energy signature of flowers, gems or other healing substances that have been captured in water and preserved

facet: the natural face of a crystal or the cut face of a gemstone

Feng Shui: the ancient Chinese art of placement

gem water: water that has been infused with crystalline energy

geode: a cavity within a rock in which crystals have grown

grounding: the connection of the body's energy to the energy of the Earth

healing: the process of restoring physical, mental, emotional or spiritual wellbeing

healing crisis: a strong and unpleasant reaction to healing, which should pass within 24–48 hours, usually triggered by a large release of unhelpful substances or energies from the body

Higher Self: an aspect of the self that remains peaceful and detached from life's dramas

homeostasis: a natural rebalancing process in the body

inclusion: material that became trapped within a crystal as it was forming

intuition: inner wisdom, or inner teaching, which gives a sense of "knowing"

Kabbalah: an ancient Jewish mystical tradition

karma: the belief that the human soul carries the impressions of experiences – good and bad – from lifetime to lifetime; karmic experiences can be repeated in different incarnations, and the individual needs to clear those karmic patterns that are blocking progress

kinesiology: a muscle-testing procedure that can be used to discover what strengthens and what weakens the body's energy

Kundalini: a strong rising energy, normally dormant at the base of the spine. Hindus visualize Kundalini Shakti as a serpent goddess; when aroused, she uncoils and rises through the column of the chakras to the crown in her quest to unite with her consort, Lord Shiva – their union leads to an expansion in consciousness.

lattice: the repeating geometric pattern of atoms that make up a crystalline structure

Law of Attraction: the belief that thoughts are powerful and creative, drawing those situations and things that are most dwelled upon

life-force energy: subtle energy that is also called chi, prana or universal energy

Lo Shu Key: a square grid containing nine squares that demonstrate the way chi energy flows, according to Feng Shui principles; also referred to as the Bagua or Pa kua

lustre: the way in which a crystal reflects the light

massive: a crystal that forms in chunks rather than having a visible crystalline structure

meridian: an energy channel or flow that runs close to the surface of the skin

microcrystalline: tiny crystals that are too small to see with the naked eye

mindfulness: the practice of keeping the mind entirely focused upon whatever you are doing in the present moment

mineral: naturally formed inorganic material with a crystalline structure

Mohs Scale of Hardness: a test of mineral hardness

mudra: a specific and meaningful hand position with roots in Buddhist, Hindu and Jain traditions

New Age: the astrological Age of Aquarius; astrological ages last 2,160 years, and it is believed that the Age of Aquarius we are now entering heralds a time of spiritual awakening and evolution

octahedron: a three-dimensional geometric shape with eight sides

opaque: a substance that blocks the passage of light and cannot be seen through

oracle card: a card used for guidance or divination

pendulum: a weight, such as a crystal, suspended on a chain or string, which is used for dowsing or healing purposes

pentagram: a five-pointed star, which is an ancient mystical and magical symbol

prana: the Sanskrit term for subtle energy

programming: the process of imprinting information into a crystal, usually clear quartz

quantum physics: a branch of physics that explores the nature and behaviour of sub-atomic particles in the creation of matter

quartz family: a large group of crystals whose members all share the same basic chemical formula of silicon dioxide SiO_2

radio frequency (RF): the part of the electromagnetic spectrum used in telecommunications and emitted by telephone masts, mobile phones and other radio devices

Rays: the seven coloured Rays that are believed to carry the purest expression of divine light

record keeper: a crystal with triangular-shaped markings, which is believed to hold programmed information; record-keeper markings are mostly found in clear quartz, ruby and sapphire

resonance: the way in which one item, such as a crystal, influences the vibration of another, bringing its frequency into convergence with its own

rock: used generally to refer to the minerals that form the Earth's crust; also used to describe aggregates comprising more than one mineral

scrying: gazing into a reflective surface to gain psychic insights and impressions

Seal of Solomon: a six-pointed star formed of two intersecting equilateral triangles, also called the Star of David; this ancient design is believed to have been given by God to King Solomon, engraved upon a ring

shielding: an energy used to create a barrier for the purpose of protection

smudge stick: a bundle of dried herbs used for cleansing purposes

smudging: the act of cleansing using smoke from a smudge stick

soul star chakra: a transpersonal chakra located above your head, which moderates the energy coming in from the cosmos

Spirit Guide: a non-physical being that has a supportive role in providing spiritual guidance for an individual

spiritual guidance: messages and advice conveyed by non-physical beings such as Spirit Guides or angels; guidance may come in a variety of forms, including words, images or synchronicity

Star of David: a six-pointed star formed of two intersecting equilateral triangles – a sacred symbol within the Jewish faith; also called the Seal of Solomon

stellar gateway chakra: a transpersonal chakra located at the top of the aura, which receives energy from the cosmos

subtle bodies: the layers of the energy field or aura that surround the physical body

subtle energy: energy that can only be sensed via extrasensory perception

synchronicity: the way in which meaningful things happen seemingly by coincidence

talisman: a lucky charm or amulet

termination: the natural point of a crystal

tetrahedron: a three-dimensional geometric shape with four sides

translucent: a substance that is not clear but enables some light to pass through

transparent: a substance that is clear, enabling the passage of light

transpersonal chakra: a chakra that is located off the physical body

tumblestone: a smoothly rounded crystal with a polished appearance

vibration: the frequency, or movement pattern and speed, of energy; low vibrations have longer, slower wavelengths, high vibrations have shorter, faster wavelengths. The range of measurable frequencies is shown on the electromagnetic spectrum, but the term also describes the nature of subtle energies that are not currently measurable

violet flame: a non-physical purifying fire believed to be the gift of the Ascended Master St Germain

visualization: the use of the imagination to form pictures in the mind's eye

yang: the masculine force of the universe that underpins Traditional Chinese Medicine

yin: the feminine force of the universe that underpins Traditional Chinese Medicine

Index of Crystals

Index

Picture Credits

Alamy Stock Photo Derek Anderson 228r, 264b; Jack Barr 160br; Science Photo Library 160al, 184l; Howard West 218r; World History Archive 260b; Björn Wylezich 252a.

Dreamstime.com Anakondasp 232b; Annausova75 194l; Mehmet Gokhan Bayhan 240l, 252cb, 288b; Briancweed 264c; Zbynek Burival 208r; Chemival 210r; Chernetskaya 174crb; Claudianass7 236b; Joaquin Corbalan 258al; Costin79 264a; Daniel127001 174l, 198l, 258ar, 278l; Eastmanphoto 214r; Efesan 222l, 280r; Peter Hermes Furian 194cr; Gozzoli 190cr, 216l; Haotian 202al; Hapelena 248l; Infinityphotostudio 242a; Bohuslav Jelen 194br, 198r, 234b, 238b, 240r, 282r; Jeyaprakash Maria 190al; Jochenschneider 178, 188br; Dana Kenneth Johnson 292l; Sergei Karpukhin 216r; Ekaterina Kriminskaya 188cr, 222r, 248r, 250b, 258b, 262b, 278ar; Nika Lerman 234a; Anna Lurye 260a; Stefan Malloch 230l; Mauserx75 232ar; Onkinnaree Metra 266a; Ruslan Minakryn 174ar, 186l, 224br, 238al, 244l, 246r, 268r, 282l; Mirecca 272r; Mrreporter 176l, Mvorobiev 170r, 196l, 268l; Andrey Nasonov 236a; Nastya22 174br, 200l, 202b, 290l; Nastya81 192, 262a; Aleksandr Nikolaev 196r; Notwishinganymore 169r, 171r; Martin Novak 280l; Andriy Olkhovyy 166br; OTWphotography 212al; Seahorsepics 232al; Tatyanaego 186r; Fabrizio Troiani 250c; TRStudio 250a, 286l; Jiri Vaclavek 244r, 254l; Vvoevale 188l, 194ar, 218l, 220a, 220b, 224ar, 226l, 226r, 238ar, 254r, 276r, 278br, 290r, 292r; Vyacheslav Tyulin 276l; Maximilian W 188ar; Wanouwawa123 208l; Wattophotos Uk 170l; Björn Wylezich 234c, 252ca.

Getty Images benedek 284l; Ron Evans 160ar, 224l; Siede Preis 180l.

iStock halock 270c; Jessica Lahoud 57; Minakryn Ruslan 190br; simarts 165; SunChan 270b; Vilotti 230r; Vvoevale 212b.

Lauren D'Silva 9ar, 149b, 151b, 166bl, 176r, 180r, 182l, 182r, 200r, 202ar, 204ar, 204cr, 204b, 266c, 272l.

Octopus Publishing Group 246l, 270a.

Science Photo Library Gary Cook, Visuals Unlimited 212ar; Natural History Museum, London 214l, 266b; Science Stock Photography 206.

Shutterstock Creative Alexei A 256l; Dafinchi 256r; Imfoto 284r; Andy.LIU 288al; Alejandro Lafuente Lopez 204l; Ruslan Minakryn 288ar; olpo 286r; Roy Palmer 160bl, 228l, 274l, 274r; photo-world 210l; Julian Popov 252b; Reload Design 174cra; Albert Russ 190bl; Stellar Gems 242b; Tim2473 184r; verbaska 224cr.

Wikimedia Commons James St. John (CC by 2.0) 190ar.

Acknowledgements

The Goddess Brigid and the Muses knew I would be writing this book before I did and inspired me throughout its creation.

A big thank you to those teachers who set my feet firmly upon the crystal path so many moons ago. Gratitude is due to my husband, Steve Deeks-D'Silva, for his support; to my grown-up children, for being my cheerleaders; and to my dog, for keeping me grounded and reminding me when it is dinner time! I am also grateful to my clients, students and workshop participants, whose enthusiasm motivates me to keep exploring this beautiful subject. I'd also like to thank the team at Octopus, especially Natalie Bradley, for inviting me to write this book, and Clare Churly, who has patiently guided me through the publishing process. Lastly, I give thanks to the Crystal Kingdom for being my touchstone through life's twists and turns over the last 20-something years.

About the Author

Lauren D'Silva has been using crystals for healing and spiritual development for over 20 years. She is a teacher with three decades of qualified experience and is founder of Touchstones School of Crystal Therapy, which provides training and professional development for crystal therapists. Students travel from all over the world to study with her. Lauren served as the Chair of the Affiliation of Crystal Healing Organisations (ACHO), the main body representing crystal healing in the UK, from 2014 to 2020. Her healing practice is based in Wales, UK. She also works with international clients via the internet.

www.laurendsilva.co.uk
www.crystal-therapy.co.uk

Also Available

Godsfield Companion: Chakras
Godsfield Companion: Mindfulness
Godsfield Companion: Yoga